HOW TO SHOOT THE LONGBOW

HUGH D. H. SOAR

HOW TO SHOOT THE LONGBOW

A GUIDE FROM HISTORICAL AND APPLIED SOURCES

WESTHOLME
Yardley

For those with whom I have shared the shooting line

Westholme Publishing, LLC
904 Edgewood Road
Yardley, Pennsylvania 19067
Visit our Web site at www.westholmepublishing.com

First Printing March 2015
10 9 8 7 6 5 4 3 2 1
ISBN: 978-1-59416-213-8
Also available as an eBook.

Printed in the United States of America

Contents

Introduction

On the greensward, somewhere in England, an archery beginner stands nervously facing his coach.

The coach has helped many a newcomer and is familiar with the problems that may occur. He has identified the eye with which his beginner will find it most advantageous to aim and introduced him to the equipment. Now he will make sure the budding archer is standing tall and is properly lined up. He has shown him how and where to fit the arrow and to place his fingers correctly in order to pull back the string.

The coach is familiar with those who—having pulled back the string and bent the bow—find themselves unable to release it, so he encourages his pupil to pull back a little way and shoot into the grass just in front of him a few times.

Since a picture is worth a thousand words, the coach then takes a similar bow and demonstrates the position he wishes his pupil to adopt. The big moment has arrived. The beginner, striving to remember what has been said, exerts himself and bends the bow.

Here we have a picture of an activity which has taken place for hundreds of years, the experienced instructing the newcomer.

If we tune our ears to the past we can hear them: "Pull it to thine ear.". . . "Lay thy body in the bow.". . . "Shoot wholly together." . . . "Fix your eye on the Mark." . . . "Do not let your arm drop." The voices echo down through the centuries—so just how have we reached this point? Come with me and I shall tell you.

———————

We know the bow is of great antiquity, and often ponder how it was first invented. Early man would have had no experience and little tuition, he would have settled into a style of shooting which felt comfortable and moreover got the required results. We have only to observe those indigenous peoples who still use the bow to see that there is both variation and similarity in their technique. A great deal depends on hunting practice and the power of the bow; generally we find that there is much stalking involved, until the shot is made at relatively short range.

Archaeological finds such as that of "Ötzi the iceman" whose body with his archery equipment intact was recovered from the Australian/Italian Alps, have extended our knowledge of the bow and its accoutrements by some 5000 years. Through this chance find we have been provided with a unique practical snapshot of both Neolithic bowyery and arrow making. Cave drawings within the French Dordogne region and elsewhere provide useful, if simple, examples of early shooting technique, methods of hunting and, to some limited extent, warfare. We therefore have a tantalizing snapshot of how Ötzi might perhaps have used his equipment and are able to supplement the knowledge already gained from the study of Ishi, the California Indian, whose method of building bows and arrows and whose hunting technique proved so helpful to our understanding of the techniques of early hunter gatherers.

Since people do not fundamentally change, no doubt there were, even in the distant past, those who were ready to advise on the best methods of shooting—even if their advice, as today, was not always welcome

With the advent of writing came a huge change, as those who felt they were sufficiently knowledgeable committed their advice to paper; and there are manuscripts available to us today from ancient peoples who gloried in the use of the bow and laid down strict criteria for the training of young people in all aspects of its use. We will leave the examination of such fascinating insights to others however, since the subject of this book is the longbow, and our task is to investigate how, over the centuries, the advice and training have changed—or not.

Although originally closely tied to the twin aspects of hunting and warfare, shooting in the longbow always had its pleasurable aspect. Competition was encouraged, even in early times, and this is still a feature today within unsophisticated native cultures as we shall later see.

Recreational archery, and in particular the competitive element, was early recognized by martial authority as an asset to tactical military advantage, useful as a preparation for the thrust of

A medieval illustration of the martydom of St. Edmund. Note the archers drawing to the chest, and their short draw length. (*Author*)

battle. Those concerned with the development of skill were only too keen to have their young men proficient in the weapon; and many were the wagers, tacitly encouraged, that were won or lost on the Tournament field as archer strove against archer. We know of course that in accordance with the law, by the Middle Ages every young lad in England would have been tutored by his father from the age of seven, for Authority was keen to ensure a ready supply of those proficient in the use of the bow.

Those looking to the many images, engravings and paintings of archers in the past to discover their technique will find themselves puzzled. There may occasionally be some indications of how the archers shot, but equally, many of them seem to be adopting a thoroughly peculiar stance—in some cases more that of a ballet dancer than a bowman. The conclusion is that the artist has followed a recognized convention, or that he had little practical knowledge of archery. This is apparent today when those unfamiliar with the activity seek to depict archers, and succeed only in sending established exponents into paroxysms of laughter—or deep groans.

So, since historical images cannot be totally relied upon, where can we start?

If anyone is qualified to be called the father of recreational archery, then that man is Roger Ascham, author of *Toxophilus, or the Schole of Shooting*, and mentor to Queen Elizabeth I. It is his advice drawn from meticulous observation over many years which still provides the basis of instruction today.

His five precepts for "fayre shuting": the *stance*; the *nock*; the *draw*; the *hold*; and the *loose*, augmented today by the *aim* and the *follow through*, will be individually discussed in detail within the following chapters and compared with the practice recommended by both earlier and later experts in the art of archery.

How to Shoot the Longbow is intended for all who feel affinity with the bow and arrow. Within its pages the curious will learn something of the arcane world of traditional archery, both past and present, and the way that these experts, some accepted as such, others self-acknowledged, explained how the act of shooting should successfully be done.

Information has been drawn from numerous sources—some altruistic by expert archers, others by archery stockists with commercial interest at heart—and from different periods. Thus, the anonymous French author of a late medieval manuscript on French archery may rub shoulders with the equally anonymous compiler of an instruction booklet provided by a nineteenth century supplier of archery gear.

The modern archer who lays aside his recurved bow or compound weapon to explore the simplicity of stick and string, and finds unexpected challenge will, we hope, benefit from the final chapter which contains coaching advice; while the authors trust that those with appetite for the multi-faceted history of style and practice through the ages will not be disappointed with the fare provided.

Prologue: Expectations

Challenges between archers were frequent across the years and those between married men and bachelors were not uncommon. A curious example of one of these survives in an invitation to contest skill made by expatriate Englishmen at "Calez" in 1478. (Calais, in France, was an English possession at the time.)

It would seem to have taken place on August 21, St. Bartholomew's Tide, a traditional day for such tournaments in earlier times. Sadly, although the invitation is explicit of the arrangements, we are not told of the outcome.

> to our well beloved good brodyr Thomas Wrighyt, and all other bachelores beying fremen of the Staple, be thee delyvered. An it wood pleyse for your dysport and plesur upon next Thursday commynge to mete with us, of the east syde of this towne in a place called the Pane ye shall fynd a pere of pricks [marks or butts] of length beytwyxt the one and th'othere xiii xx Taylour yardes meyt out with a lyne. There the under wryten shalle meyt with alles many of your Ordyr and shote with you at the same pryks for a dynere or a supper price xiid a man. And we pray your goodly answere within xxiiii ourse
>
> Wreten at Calez the xvij Day of August.
>
> Robert Adlyn
>
> Johan Dyase
>
> Johan Elkyngton
>
> Richard Wyloby

Phelep Williamson
Robert Besters
Simon Grantham
Thomas Lane
Thomas Sharpe
Johan Wright
William Bondeman
Robert Knigyt

Assuming a yard then to be of today's value and measurement, between the two Butts would have been thirteen score (260) yards and an indication of the distance expected of longbowmen of the period.

ONE

Stance and Posture

"The first point is when a man should shoot to take suche footinge and standinge as shall be both comely to the eye and profitable to his use."
—Roger Ascham, *Toxophilus*

We have no exact knowledge of attitudes towards these important preparatory aspects of the shot in ancient times. It is possible however to gain some indication of past practices by studying those illustrations which exist. Manuscript drawings are of course likely to reflect the artist's personal perceptions and the artistic conventions of the time—which are unlikely to provide more than a general scan of actual practice. Where there is no written word in support, however, we must accept what little information they offer and comment accordingly.

One aspect seems common to all such illustrations, and that is the open stance. This can be seen in a drawing within the Luttrell Psalter[1] created in the early fourteenth century, and illustrating medieval archers at practice; it is explicit of both stance and style. Style we will return to later, but the stance as shown is open, with legs wide apart and greater weight resting on the left, forward foot; the right taking its lesser share on the ball of the foot.

Apart from one or two contemporary illustrations where it is reversed, this would seem to have been the default position as perceived in those far-off days; the body hinging forward from the hips to a greater or lesser extent—evidence for the dynamic loose which would have been expected in warfare.

In the heat of battle, archery was anything but static of course; it is interesting to notice that all but two of those archers portrayed in the eleventh century Bayeux tapestry[2] depicting the English battle of Hastings are shooting on the move. The two static bowmen are upright; one is tall, fully mail-coated and helmeted and bears four arrows in his bow hand. He is perhaps the Norman soldier in charge. The other is a small, solitary Saxon archer doing his level best to halt the advancing Norman army.

We can gain very little more knowledge of stance from these medieval illustrations and we will now leave them for the written word.

In the late fifteenth century a Frenchman with intimate knowledge of the bow and arrow set down advice for those aspiring to shooting excellence. The author of *L'art d'archerie* chose to remain anonymous, opening his treatise by declaring,

> In no book I have ever read have I ever found anything about archery, except in the book of Modus and Racio. It is [therefore] my fixed determination, as a pastime, to write down all that I have learned so as to stir up those who are willing to learn.

He adds:

> There is good and sufficient reason that these things should clearly be brought to the knowledge of men ... and as I know that many take pleasure in archery I have resolved for my amusement to write some things down.[3]

Although this manuscript was published at the end of the fifteenth century, it seems likely from the preface that the author was reflecting French archery practice at the time of that 1478 challenge between English longbowmen of Calais mentioned earlier. It has been suggested that his treatise is indicative of

English influence; and when we examine his comments upon the draw and release, it is possible that we are also reading of English archery practice at the time, or if not, then we can study the sequences knowing that those fifteenth century Calais bowmen would have known of them

Rustic bowmen under instruction, from the fourteenth century Luttrell Psalter. (*Author*)

L'art d'Archerie is in nine chapters and it is in the ninth and last that we read of the way in which the medieval Frenchman shot. Curiously there seems to have been no distinction made between shooting for distance with its dynamic and fluid stance and the more formal discipline of butt (target) shooting. The reader who is familiar with the calm preparation for the shot fundamental to modern practice, is invited to consider the following gyrations.

> You must know that there are several ways of loosing, but all depend upon two things—on the drawing hand, and on the step, of which there are three kinds, that is to say, with one, two, or three steps. The one step way is done in two ways; one is stepping forward with the foot of the bow hand side, and the other by bringing back the arm, pushing out the bow and arrow, and at the same time stepping forward with the other foot. This step straightens the arm, but it must be a long and sharp step back.
>
> The two other ways are by taking two steps and three steps. To shoot with two steps, a backward step must be taken with the hindmost foot, so that on bringing the front foot down, sufficient impetus is given to effect the loose. For the three step, the front foot is moved forward, then the bow is thrust forward as explained above, and the hinder foot is brought back in such a way that when the arrow is released one can step forward with the front foot.

Since it is difficult to imagine how one might aim accurately using any of these methods, it would seem that the author may be referring to distance shooting. This "loosing" advice seems strange, even bizarre, to us today, but we must accept it for what it was, a five-hundred-year-old description by an expert archer of the best practice of the time. His remarks are interesting but enigmatic.

Target shooting, at 300 paces—about 240 yards—is briefly mentioned, as is Flight shooting, but neither is described in detail.

At least two of the many French archery societies trace their beginning to medieval times and at each the traditional activity seems to have been *tir aux buttes* shot at close distance. At Conde St. Libiare (Department Seine et Marne) the *Societe d'arc* formed in 1302 shot buttes at fifty meters. At Doullens (Department Somme), the *Francs Archers* formed in 1437 shot buttes at forty-five meters and *Tir a la Perche* at thirty-five meters in height. Were members of each of these ancient Clubs also shooting at targets 300 paces away? It would be interesting to know. In modern France, some town and village archery clubs with their roots in medieval times still shoot the traditional *tir a berceau* (target archery) at short distances, much as we imagine their ancestors did. It would be interesting to know what posture and stance those early archers adopted.

The longbow was almost as familiar in medieval France as it was in England. In earlier times it was a hunting weapon, and as such was known intimately to the nobility whose pleasure this was. In addition to the archery advice within the fifteenth century *l'Art d'Archerie*, we learn from the fourteenth century hunting treatise, *Book of King Modus*,[4] something of earlier medieval French archery; for here we are told that the bow had two uses—for recreation, by which is meant hunting, and for defense.

The "mysteries" of the hunting bow are first described, including the choice of string; this should be of silk, since silk is strong, stiff and hard, thus striking a heavier blow than flax or hemp. An exhortation to shoot straight follows, the archer being careful to place the arrow against the bow with the feathers lying flat—otherwise it is said, the arrow will not hit the mark. Thirdly the arrow should be drawn with three fingers, holding the nock (string notch) between the first and second fingers.

It is advised that the point of the arrow should not be too heavy and that the fletchings be cropped and low; however, if a heavy head is used, then the feathers should be correspondingly higher. We are told that when making the arrow, the shaft should be arranged in such a way that the barbs of the arrow run parallel to the nock thus avoiding damage to the hand when at full draw.

Next come the dimensions of bow and arrow. The former should be twenty-two "handfuls"—assessed as 77 inches—between nocks, and the arrow ten handfuls or 35 inches.

Thus were the 'mysteries' revealed to the pupils of King Modus. However, there was another practitioner of hunting in the offing. Gaston Phoebus, *nom de plume* of the Comte de Fois whose contribution[5] was more revealing and whose advice was mirrored in a similar book by that notable hunter of the fifteenth century, and casualty of Agincourt, the Duke of York.

Gaston Phoebus advised that a sportsman's bow should be of yew or boxwood, and measure twenty palms—assumed to be a slightly more manageable 70 inches between nocks. When braced there should be a "handful," perhaps 3 1/2 inches, between string and belly of bow.

The arrow length is as that recommended by Roy Modus, but dimensions of the head are given. It should be four fingers broad—about 3 inches—and four fingers in length—about five inches.

Gaston Phoebus provides a mystery since he speaks of the English "turkie bow," a description which evidently fits a longbow but appears to distinguish it as apart from the conventional weapon, suggesting that this was the special name given to hunting bows. We know that the hunting weapon was lighter in draw-weight than the war-bow and with its silken string and perhaps better finish perhaps sufficiently distinct to have a separate identity. It is equally possible that "turkie bow" was at one time the colloquial term for the longbow. We can only speculate.

Since hunting was the favored recreation of French nobility, advice is given for shooting when an archer is at "stable stand"—that is when standing motionless by a tree or in a thicket. He should place himself downwind of the prey and, when he views a deer approaching, he should first keep hidden from sight and cautiously raise his bow upright, holding the drawing hand with arrow nocked directly before his face. If the animal approaches without stopping the archer should silently and cautiously extend his arms and draw his bow "softly" so that he is at full draw before the prey reaches him.

His bow should be "weak and gentle," so that he may partially draw without difficulty. Then, as the deer is passing he should draw the bowstring to his right ear, and, as the deer passes he should follow it with his bow, drawing and redrawing the shaft until, having assured his aim he lets fly with a sharp and steady loose.

Although hunting was an important activity both for sport, and the local economy, as we have seen French archery had other recreational forms; both butt and flight shooting were popular, as was a form of *tir a la perche*. These then were the ways in which the early French shot.

Moving forward in time we meet with Roger Ascham whose book *Toxophilus, the Schole or Partitions of Shooting*[6] has been the "Bible" of archers since its publication in 1544. Although mainly concerned with practical advice, Ascham was at pains to promote "comeliness" in shooting.

While dismissing himself as a "poor archer," he rails against those who prepare their shot in a haphazard manner. "The best shooting is always the most comlye shooting." This he stresses must come from a correct stance, which he calls "footinge and standinge" which "shall be both comely to the eye and profitable to use." However, "a man must not go hastily to it, for that is rashnesse, nor yet make so much to do about it, for that is a curiosity." He defines the ideal position

> the one foote must not stand too far from the other, lest he stoop too much, which is unseemly, nor yet too near togeth-

Hunting deer with a bow and crossbow. (*Author*)

er lest he stand too straight up, for so a man shall neither use
his strength well, nor yet stand steadfastly

Having set down the parameters he then comments that the
"mean betwixt both must be kept, a thing more pleasant to
behold when it is done, than easy to be taught how it should be
done." Many of today's coaches faced with the "awkward
squad"—those to whom physical coordination is a mystery—
must echo his feelings.

Ascham sets great store by the stance, seeing it as integral to
preparation for the draw. Of this preparation he is most caustic,
listing some of the faults he has seen, and they are many. "One
shooteth his head forward as though he would bite the marke
another stareth with eyes as though they would fly out; another
winketh with one eye and looketh with the other [the suggestion here seems to be that shooting with only the master eye

open is not yet a feature of sixteenth century archery] another biteth his lippes, another holdeth his neck awrye." And so it goes.

As we shall later see, he is even more scathing of his fellow archers when drawing the string.

Comments about stance in the sixteenth century would not be complete without the mention of one strange happening. A passage in Raphael Holinshed's sixteenth-century *Chronicles* mentions that on one occasion when King Henry VIII was at a May festival, where people had come to see him shoot—"for he could shoot as far and as well as any of his guard"—a man came from the crowd and asked to be allowed to show his shooting to the king. On being given permission it is said the man put his "foot in his bosom" and standing on the other foot gave a very good display of shooting. The king was amused by this and rewarded him for doing so. He was known afterwards as "foot in bosom."

Walter Michael Moseley, a well-respected eighteenth-century man of letters and an archer himself, records an attempt to recreate this event in his *Essay on Archery*.[7] He was sufficiently curious to experiment with what he thought could be the method; raising his left leg and turning the toes a little inward he placed the middle of the bow against his foot, at the same time holding it close to the bow with his left hand to prevent it from slipping. He did this successfully and was able to draw a heavy bow without much difficulty. Whether this was the original posture of course is open to question.

Henry VIII was noted for his enjoyment and love of archery. He was responsible for establishing the Guild or Fraternity of Saint George,[8] by granting a charter of incorporation in August 1537. Guilds of archers, gathered for practice and mutual pleasure were common in the rural communities but this was rather different for it was exclusive, with members drawn from the ruling class and having important privileges.

Although concerned with sport, Henry had more fundamental matters in mind. Those fortunate few who were elected to membership of the Guild were to be responsible for *"the better increase of the defence of the Realm"* while maintaining the *"Science and Feat of Shooting in Longbow, Crossbow and Handgun."*

They were allowed to shoot at "all manner of Marks, and Butts and the Game of Popinjay," and shooting at game birds was permitted as well. They were privileged to keep their bows and guns in their residences, although with the proviso that while there, although their servants might carry these, they were not permitted to use them.

Members could hunt or shoot wherever they pleased, in the "Realm of England, Ireland, Calais, and the Welsh Marches" excepting only the vicinity of any castle or residence at which the king might be staying. An important privilege was exemption from the charge of homicide should a passer-by be slain while the member was at practice, always accepting that the ground was recognized for archery, and that "fast" (stand fast) had been called.

The Fraternity of Saint George evolved over the centuries into the Honourable Artillery Company, an important gunnery regiment in the modern British army and one with many battle honors.

A second Tudor archery Society, and another with a royal beginning, was Prince Arthur's Knights,[9] originally an obscure archery group with vague roots associated with young Prince Arthur, elder son of Henry VII, heir to the English throne, and reputed to be a fine archer. So fine a bowman was young Arthur that after his premature death, others who were deemed to match his skill were associated with his name.

Circumstantial evidence suggests that the Society which bears his name was confirmed by patent of the king in or about 1542–43; it is said to have been formed in order to allow citizens of London to get together annually to shoot. Evidence for its existence is contained within a little book written by Richard Robinson, a minor Elizabethan author. If accurate, the date of its founding may have been linked to the belief that the legendary King Arthur died in AD 543, 1543 thus being his millennium.

This original Society petered out at an unknown date, to be revived or reformed many years later in 1578 during the reign of Queen Elizabeth I as a quasi-Arthurian Society; individual members taking the names of Arthurian knights. In his book

Richard Robinson lists the names of these knights together with the initials of members "owning" them. Tantalizingly their names are not given and we cannot identify members. Just two are known for certain: Thomas Smith, Farmer of Customs (chief Customs Officer), who was "Prince Arthur," and Alderman Hugh Offley, who was "Sir Lancelot."

It is possible that some of those forming the Society were connected with units of the City of London Trained Band, also with City Aldermen. Members are known to have practiced archery on Mile End fields in East London where roving Marks were set. The Society survived into the seventeenth century, although it seems to have deteriorated into just a mere fairground amusement.

We now move on into the seventeenth century and first to the military archer; for although the bow was obsolescent as a weapon, and had been for a generation, there were a vociferous few for whom it remained viable. Among these was William Neade, an ancient archery entrepreneur whose arguments had persuaded King Charles I of the virtue of combining bow and pike, to produce what he called the "Double Armed Man."[10] Neade's technique, evolved to allow this, required an open stance with the heel of the pike resting against the right foot and the left stretched well forward to balance the forward weight of the pike. The bow arm held the pike, to which the bow was attached by a form of universal joint. After shooting, ideally the bow was un-braced and held against the pike. If ever used in the heat of battle though, when push of pike was necessary it might have been an encumbrance and a difficult weapon to master.

Although there is some slight evidence for the double armed man during the English Civil War he quickly faded into obscurity.

While the seventeenth century saw the ultimate demise of the military weapon, it also saw the emergence of the true recreational longbow. While the object of some of those who wrote in its favor was to belatedly bring it back into military use, others who were more pragmatically inclined recognized it as a means for pleasure and proclaimed it as such.

Second-to-none in this regard was Gervase Markham (1568?–1637), a man with intimate earlier knowledge both of warfare in the Low Countries and of the bow. While he may have had some forlorn hope of a resurgence of interest, as witness his dedication to one William Trumball, Muster-Master Generall of all England, his book *The Art of Archery*[11] is concerned with use of the bow for pleasure.

There being little or no concept of copyright in those far off days, Markham drew blatantly from Ascham's *Toxophilus* adding his own gloss where he felt it appropriate. The result is an interesting seventeenth century "update" of sixteenth century practice. He restates Ascham's comments about the stance but adds advice about the effect of weather.

> A skilful archer will learn to know the nature of the wind and will measure in his mind how much it will alter his shoot either in length or in straight shooting and so change his standing. . . . In a side wind you must stand somewhat crosse into the wind for you shall shoot the surer.

He also draws attention to the need for a clean shaft:

> when you have taken your footinge then look to your shaft that neither wet nor earth be left upon it, looke also to the head lest it have had any stripe [damage] at the last shoot, for a stripe against a stone many times will both spoil the head, crook [make crooked] the shaft and hurt the feather, the least of which will make a man lose his length.

Markham is perhaps unique in listing the ideal contents of the "compact pouch" which he advises every archer to carry by his side: "A Fyle, a [sharpening] Stone, a Hurfish-skin" (perhaps the rough skin of a shark), and "a cloth to wipe his shafts clean." Oddly however he does not include beeswax for the string. He concludes,

> Who so marks his weather diligently, and keeps his Standing justly, holds his nock truly, drawes and looseth equally and keepes his compass certainly can never miss his length. These

things thus known and observed, then ought our Archer compare the weather and his Footing together and with discretion measure them, so that whatsoever the weather shall take away from his shoot, the same shall his just [proper] Footing restore.

The seventeenth century saw the beginning of several important archery societies. The earliest among them was the Society of Finsbury Archers, thought to have been formed prior to 1636 when reference is made to them in the records of the Honourable Artillery Company,[12] a body with which they had close association. Finsbury Fields was their shooting ground; for although roving marks were present there in large numbers, the Fields were used also by archers shooting at target and butt.

It was the practice of the society to pass responsibility for its proper running to two Stewards, and these were elected annually at a feast, held for many years at the Rosemary Branch, a well known eating house at the northern end of Finsbury Fields.

It also elected a Marshall, a principal officer who held the title for life. Most notable was Sir William Wood. The society, of which we shall learn more later, ceased operating in the middle of the eighteenth century when building development reduced the land available in Finsbury Fields for shooting.

King Charles II was fond of archery and encouraged its use as a recreation. It gained in popularity during his reign when two other important societies were formed. First were the Archers at Scorton,[13] a small Yorkshire town where in 1673 a group of gentlemen gathered together to a contest annually for a silver arrow. The first archer to pierce a spot in the exact center of the target became captain and gained custody of the arrow for a year. He was also expected to provide the venue and arrangements for the succeeding meeting. It would be interesting to know whether any of their members drew support from Markham's advice.

After more than three hundred years this is the oldest sporting event to have been continually held in Britain, and provides the oldest sporting trophy to have been annually contested for that period of time, since although the Kilwinning Archers in Scotland predate the Scorton there have been breaks in its activ-

ities. In passing the origin of the
"Antient Scorton Silver Arrow" has
been the subject of speculation, as have
the rules and regulations of the society
which are similar to those of the
Finsbury Archers.[14]

Scotland is a country with a strong
archery tradition, and it provided the
second society of note during Charles
II's reign, for in 1676 an influential
group of Scottish patriots, noblemen,
and gentlemen met "for the purpose of
encouraging the Noble and Useful
recreation of Archery, for many years
neglected." They were to be known as
the Royal Company of Archers,[15] for
they ultimately became the official
bodyguard of the Monarch.

A seventeenth-century
archer. Note the low
drawing hand used to ele-
vate the arrow—probably
for distance shooting.
(*Author*)

They oversaw the major Scottish archery contests and quickly
became regarded as the premier archery organization in
Scotland, a position unsuccessfully disputed by fellow archers
belonging to the Ancient Society of Kilwinning Archers who
claimed an origin in the fifteenth century and thus pride of
place.

In 1704 the Royal Company was granted a Charter of
Corporation by Queen Anne. This allowed them "perpetual
access to all public butts, places and pasturages legally allotted for
shooting arrows with the bow, each at random distances (roving)
and at measured (target and butt) distances." In consideration of
this permission, the queen and her successors were to be provided, in perpetuity—and upon their request, with a pair of arrows
known as the "Reddendo." In archery terms a "pair" is actually
three. In 1822 the Company achieved its greatest honor: King
George IV permitted members to act as the sovereign's bodyguard for Scotland. Members of The Royal Company have close
ties with a senior English club, the Woodmen of Arden, with
whom they hold periodic meetings.

Archery with the recreational longbow, so popular among the upper class during the reign of Charles II, diminished significantly after his death in 1687. Although certain societies survived, including the Society of Finsbury Archers, the Scorton Antient Silver Arrow Meeting, and the Royal Company of Archers of Scotland, the pastime did not generally revive until once more favored by royalty in the late eighteenth century.

Those who wrote on the subject at that time seem to have been more interested in the history of the bow than in its practical purpose and the way in which it should be shot. In a lecture to the Archaeological Society in 1783, recorded in Volume VII of *Archaeologia*, the Honourable Daines Barrington spoke eloquently of the importance of the bow's use in warfare but offered sparse information about its recreational role. With this role firmly re-established however, Walter Michael Moseley was more explicit in his *Essay on Archery*,[16] although contributing nothing to the matter of posture or stance, of recreational archery he comments:

> It is attended with no cruelty. It sheds no innocent blood nor does it torture harmless animals. It is not necessarily laborious and may be discontinued when it becomes fatiguing. Archery as a recreation is an exercise adapted to every age and every degree of strength.

What better commentary could there be with which to end this chapter.

TWO

Lessons from Our Predecessors

"One foot must not stand too far from the other, lest he stoop too much, which is unbecoming; nor yet too near the other, lest he should stand too straight up, for so a man shall neither use his strength well, nor yet stand steadfastly."

—Thomas Roberts, *The English Bowman*

With a new century opening, in 1802 it was Thomas Roberts, an active member of the Toxophilite Society, who took things forward. His important and lengthy work, *The English Bowman*[1] describes the posture and stance of the eighteenth century archer in detail, drawing on a portrait, seemingly from life, of an eminent eighteenth century archer standing in readiness to shoot. The name of this example of excellence is not given, but from his stance we can clearly see what was believed right for good shooting at the time. It is possible that it was Sir Ashton Lever.

From penciled notes found in his own copy of *The English Bowman*, we have interesting detail of Roberts's personal performance on The Woodmen of Arden's grounds in Warwickshire where, with permission, he regularly shot.

Since Roberts is the first to contribute any significant information about recreational archery since Ascham, two hundred and fifty years earlier, we can look in detail at his writing. He opens by quoting from the poet Richard Niccols[2] whose poem *London's Artillery* (1616) is about the Honourable Artillery Company and describes the proper position for an archer of those times:

> Setting his left leg somewhat forth before
> His arrow with his right hand nocking sure,
> Not stooping, nor not standing straight upright.
> Then, with his left hand a little above his sight
> Stretching his arm out, with an easy strength,
> To draw an arrow of a yard in length.

Roberts goes on to build on this outline.

> The archer should not oppose [present] his foot but his side to the Mark, by which means he not only eyes [sees] it better, but also gives scope to his drawing arm.
> By laying the body into the bow, is meant the inclining of the head a little forward; but the archer must bend as little as possible from the waist, and must beware of inclining to his left side. This inclining forward not only enables him to bring his bow-arm more in a direct line with his drawing arm, and so see his mark better, but at the same time frees his chest, coat and hat—which latter should be turned up on the shaft side—from the string. [These were the days when archers wore shooting jacket, waistcoat and hat.]
> When the bow arm is brought [pushed] forward the string will not catch the upper edge of the bracer [worn of course on the coat sleeve]. His knees should be straight, not bent, and his hams [thighs] being extended but with an easy firmness. He should keep his feet flat and firm upon the ground without resting more on one leg than the other for a partial bearing on one leg tends to render him unsteady and so disturb his whole action [no mention of the effect of weather here] although it has been observed that the most perfect archer of

this day [name unspecified] was accustomed to place a little more stress on the right than on the left leg.

His left leg should be advanced a little forward of his right and the outside of the former almost parallel to the right whilst the other may keep its usual position. The heels may be about six inches apart.

Much of Roberts commentary comes from observing the illustration of the archer, possibly Sir Ashton Lever, forming the frontispiece to his book. He considers that it shows all the characteristics he has outlined. Qualities of strength, ease, coolness, resolution, dexterity and vigor, each of which he considers necessary to the perfect shot. No doubt Sir Ashton would have been pleased.

Roberts concludes by commenting that the young archer should approach his shooting with coolness and attention, "for haste and too great an eagerness are qualities in an archer which must be got rid of before he can arrive at any degree of excellence in the art." A worthy precept, and one as relevant today as it was two hundred years ago.

Among the more important of those Societies influenced by Roberts were the Toxophilites formed in 1781 through the efforts of Sir Ashton Lever and Thomas Waring, his business secretary.

A group of fourteen archers, including one or two of the now defunct Finsbury Archers, gathered together to form the nucleus of the society, meeting initially and shooting at Leicester House, home of Mr. Waring. Never having a large membership but comfortable with some sixty archers, it had difficulty in finding a suitable shooting ground, settling for many years in Regents Park, London. It is now happily established at a permanent ground in Burnham Beeches, Buckinghamshire.

Historically there had been, and still was, close affinity between the Toxophilites and the Honourable Artillery Company and this became even closer in 1784 when a number of members, wishing to shoot on the Artillery Company grounds, were admitted to the company as full members acting as a "flank division"[3] mustering with the company and attending parades fully dressed and equipped, including bayonets and gaiters. Drawn from the Toxophilites, this group operated independently; and at national meetings provided a separate team.

The Prince of Wales, later George IV, became patron of the society in 1787, conferring upon it the title "Royal." As the premier English archery society the "Royal Tox" as it is affectionately known today, had for long been the arbiter of archery matters in the United Kingdom before the gradual take-over of this responsibility by the Grand National Archery Society in the 1950s.

A second important eighteenth century society, now defunct, was the Royal British Bowmen.[4] Formed in 1787 by Sir Foster and Lady Cunliffe of Acton Park in North Wales it began as a gathering of social equals in the neighborhood, expanding later to draw from those classes in the English border counties. It was quickly patronized by the Prince of Wales from whom it acquired its royal title. It has an enigmatic origin, for there is circumstantial evidence to suggest its formation by Lady Cunliffe[5] through intercession with her husband, after a visit from a certain unnamed but influential gentleman, thought by some to have been Sir Ashton Lever, who taught her to shoot.

The first meeting took place on February 27, 1787; and the society continued shooting until 1794 when matters were interrupted by the Napoleonic War. Sporadic meetings held in 1802 fizzled out, but shooting resumed from 1819 and continued uninterrupted until 1880. The Society was unusual for its time in admitting women as equals from its beginning.

The R.B.B., as it was known colloquially, is well documented, and surviving records give an unusual glimpse into the life of the eighteenth century social set where as much emphasis was placed upon the feasting and dancing as on the shooting. We have an account of many of the meetings and the arrangements were impressive.

The day began with assembly in the Great Hall of the House, followed by a march, two by two, to the shooting ground, preceded by a full military band playing a lively piece composed especially for the occasion. Once there they were greeted by a twenty-one gun royal salute. Deafened by the noise, shooting then began. When all was over they marched back, the band now playing *Here the Conquering Hero Comes*, escorting the victors crowned with laurel leaves.

Shooting was nominally at ninety yards for men and sixty yards for women, although these varied according to the whim of the organizers and the weather. Evidently shorter distances were also shot, since silver arrows were purchased for thirty yard shooting. Scores were probably consistent with archery of the time, when aiming was anything but an exact science. Thus, in 1791 ladies shot fifty arrows at seventy yards—a Miss Newcome winning with just sixteen hits and scoring fifty-four; while the men shot at 120 yards, with Sir Foster Cunliffe taking the laurel leaves, having achieved eight hits and forty scored.

Although a standard target was used, in 1821 a new form was adopted in which two vertical lines of the width of the gold were drawn; hits within these lines scored an additional point, thus making comparison with other contemporary societies impossible.

A third important eighteenth century society, formed in 1785, was the Woodmen of Arden.[6] A small group of gentlemen meeting initially in the grounds of the Bull Inn at Meriden in Warwickshire, they were fortunate to attract the interest of the Earl of Aylesford, himself a notable archer, who graciously allowed them shooting rights on a field belonging to his estate. This field, now enhanced by a splendid eighteenth century hall, has been their home ever since. Successive Lords Aylesford have held the title and office of Lord Warden since the inception of the society, while for almost 150 years the family Thompson provided bows for the members.

The Society remains all male, although wives, sisters and daughters are welcomed on occasion to shoot as "lassies of the forest." An album of individual photographic portraits of every nineteenth shooting member exists and is thought to be a unique collection.

The Woodmen have close affinity with the Royal Company of Archers with whom they have held triennial matches since July 1878.

Following Thomas Roberts and his *The English Bowman* chronologically is Thomas Waring the Younger. With paternal influence, as might be expected, he had views on posture and stance. Within his *Treatise on Archery*,[7] his opening comments are selective and unusual:

> Madame Bola, formerly a famous opera dancer, upon being taught the use of the bow, declared that of all the attitudes she ever studied (and surely some deference ought to be paid to the opinion of one whose life was spent in studying attitudes) she thought the position of shooting with the longbow was the most noble and graceful; certainly it is that the human figure cannot be displayed to greater advantage than when drawing the bow.

After this fulsome introduction what follows is disappointedly brief. He tells us that the only part of the front of the body to be turned towards the mark is the face; so if the mark is full south, the body should be turned towards the west, the face looking over the left shoulder.

Waring dismisses foot position in a few words. "The heels should be from four to six inches apart. The head to incline a little downward over the breast."

Archery was adopted generally by the leisured and moneyed elite as another amusement, a pleasant and convenient way of meeting friends socially. It had another advantage however; it was one of the few activities open to younger early nineteenth century women and became popular with them for that reason. Women regularly outnumbered men at the public meetings where they enjoyed both the atmosphere and the sporting challenge.

Archery societies, beside their social element with opportunity for families of equal status to mix and mingle, also offered the chance for match making, and many were the marriages resulting from encounters—by chance or engineered—on the archery field. The earlier nineteenth century clubs were in effect an outdoor extension of the drawing room. While engaging in a pleasant pursuit one met with one's peers—quite literally in some societies, since minor nobility still supported the activity.

Artisans—known dismissively as "trade"—were excluded. The rule of thumb seems to have been that if admitted through the front door then the chance of membership was reasonable. If the back door were your usual means of access then you stood no chance. One or two clubs were quite exact about exclusions; bowyers were specifically barred from both membership and from the shooting grounds.[8] A curious decision, suggesting perhaps that some bow makers did not regard themselves as "trade" and needed to be reminded of the fact—or were they perceived to have an unfair advantage in skill, technique, or equipment? The decision could have been a source of embarrassment however, since one particular bow maker was not only a respected and valued member of his club, but had twice become national champion. Not only that, but his bows were particularly prized and it is possible that at least one gentleman owned and shot a bow of his making. This man was Peter Muir, bow maker to the Royal Company. It would have been interesting had he chosen to apply for membership.

During the greatest popularity of the pastime, almost every town of note in Britain had its archery club or society. In 1865 ninety such were recorded in the *Archers Register*[9] and many more who chose not to advertise themselves would also have existed.

Although there were still several clubs exclusive to men, and one or two that only admitted women, early Victorian archery was largely an extended family affair with the subsequent picnic a dominant feature for some.

While the young lads had their role as "arrow boys," picking up spent shafts for portly gentlemen and ladies in restrictive crinolines, they and their sisters were encouraged to shoot for special awards, and there was at least one juvenile archery club established.

In the earlier years of the century shooting was largely for relaxation and pleasure, with club competition and, beginning in 1844, the Grand National Meeting, an annual event marking the extent of competitive interest. As the century advanced, however, competition became more acceptable, and a second major public archery meeting was added to the scene in 1854, the Leamington and Midland Counties Meeting.[10]

Clubs welcomed visits from their neighbors, and competitions were well attended. Occasionally at the larger clubs there would be a guest appearance by a notable archery figure, and this would bring crowds literally by the trainload to watch their shooting. Betting on competitors was rife, although officials tried hard to curb it.

Monetary prizes added interest, particularly among the better shots—although they protested that their objectives were in no way mercenary. However, at least one national champion was quite open about her desire to win. Mrs. Atkinson, a widow with a young family, had no qualms about accepting monetary awards to supplement her modest income.

The next attempt to influence excellence which we will examine comes from *The Young Archer's Assistant*, published in 1854 by up and coming London bowyer Thomas Aldred and written by "F.M.", a practicing archer, identified as Reverend Francis Merewether.[11]

Thomas Aldred, with partners Joseph Ainge and James Buchanan, acquired the established archery business of John and David Freeman in about 1845. It was never a successful partnership, James Buchanan was unhappy at the arrangement, and he lasted barely a year before leaving to form his own firm, followed some years later by Ainge. After this diffident start in the archery business, Aldred gave up his previous employment with a London firm of brokers and devoted himself full-time to, among other creative activities, bow and arrow making. He is unusual in that his booklet addresses its advice specifically to the aspirant young.

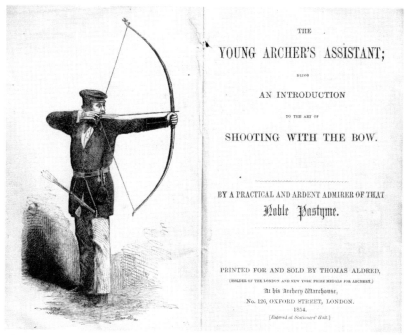

The posture as promoted in the *Young Archer's Assistant*. Note the oblique stance. (*Author*)

After quoting Ascham at some length—and in the original Tudor English which might have puzzled a young lad—Aldred's writer, if it were not he himself, tackles the *position*.

> We have now arrived at the most important point for ensuring if not proficiency, and a high state of perfection, at least grace and elegance. The system we advocate is, in respect of standing, unlike those which are laid down in most books on Archery.
>
> We object to the young archer being directed to stand sideways, in place of which we would advise that he should stand with the right foot pointed towards the target from which he is about to shoot, the left at right angles with it, the heels about six or eight inches apart, the weight of his body thrown equally on both feet, the knees to be quite straight, not bent, and the whole body, neck and head to be kept in a perpendicular position.

Any person who has been accustomed to shoot in a different position will probably consider it is a contentious one and ill adapted for exerting the strength he may possess; but this work is altogether intended for beginners. We contend that this position may as easily be acquired as any other.

The advantage it possesses, independent of appearance, is, that it more immediately calls into action and assistance the muscles of the back and breast, and, in our opinion is the only one which enables the archer to "lay his body in the Bow" i.e. to make use of the muscles of the body.

To what extent Aldred's advice influenced the young beginner is unknown of course, but many would have had older family members to advise them and it is problematical whether they would recommend what may have seemed to them an unnatural stance.

Those who sought for advice culled from an expert however had not long to wait, for twelve times National Champion Horace Ford, whose skill with the bow was plain for all to see, had published his seminal work *Archery*[12] in 1859, the year of inauguration of the Crystal Palace public meeting, replacing an unsuccessful attempt to hold a public meeting in Birmingham.

Ford devotes considerable time to "footing" as he calls it, commenting that, "there are as many varieties existing as there are archers. Certain it is that hardly any two shoot precisely in the same form and very few without some individual mannerism." Such being the case, he concludes that, "it would be venturing too far to assert that just one position is good, or any one is the best." Having said this, he offers some general rules in order to control such "mannerisms" which effectively prevent even moderate hitting, restraining them within "harmless limits" so as not to "violate all the requisites of grace and elegance." One is reminded of the sixteenth-century "foot in bosom" shooter.

Ford's concept of a good general position embodies three qualities: firmness, elasticity, and grace. "Firmness to resist the force, pressure and recoil of the bow . . . elasticity to give free play to the muscles and the needful command over them . . . and grace to render the shooter and his performance agreeable to the eyes of a spectator." This latter quality would be of particular interest to his lady readers and also to Ford himself, since he had a substantial following who turned out to watch him shoot.

Ford goes on to describe the elements of footing, commenting that legs should not be "straddled abroad . . . . As if he were preparing to withstand the blow of a battering ram." Feet should be "flat and firm on the ground, inclining a little outwards from the heels, with the toes some six inches wider apart than the heels. . . . The standing must be at right angles to the mark. Knees must be perfectly straight not bent in the slightest degree. The weight of the body must be thrown equally on both legs. In short the footing must be firm, yet at the same time easy and springy."

Ford is particularly scathing of the body bending forward from the waist, seeing this as "highly objectionable on every account." The shooter who adopts this position "requires so much wit and muscle to avoid tumbling on his nose that he has little left to help him hit the mark." That said however he advises against the opposite extreme, the "excessively upright stance." He ends by advising not to push the head forward since this can lead to a "merciless rap on the nose."

Ford has much to say about shooting in general and in later chapters we will meet him again. There is telling circumstantial evidence that his words were listened to and absorbed, since a glance at the scores made at the national meetings following the publication of his book show considerable increase over those of the years before.

Next in our trundle through the pages of those who queued to advise the archer is bowyer Frederick Henry Ayres, whose booklet, *The Handbook of Archery*[13] was produced in 1898. Although archery was no longer an obligatory social activity, there were many clubs catering both for single men and women and married couples with their young families; there was much competition between them and a wish by many to excel. Since Ayres equipment was popular he evidently felt it necessary to offer advice to those who bought his tackle.

Having opened the *Handbook* however, it may have disappointed the knowledgeable reader to see that with the exception of some disputed aspects of shooting, the contents were an exact copy of what had been written by Thomas Waring the Younger in his *Treatise on Archery, or the Art of Shooting,* some seventy years earlier. No reference here to the advice of Horace Ford or to his seminal work.

A booklet published in 1860 by A.N. Myers, proprietor of an archery warehouse, *The Archer's Guide, or Instruction for the use of the Long Bow* is equally disappointing in its repetition of Waring's work, albeit with an acknowledgment by its author "H.D.," and a change of illustration.[14]

We move now to the early twentieth century, to that giant of the archery establishment, Colonel H. Walrond and his booklet *Archery for Beginners*[15] published in 1904. Col. Walrond is the first contributor since Horace Ford forty years before, to examine preparation for the shot in technical detail. We will look at his wise advice for preparing the stance.

> The shooter should stand on the Mark [the shooting line] in front of the target (from which he is shooting), sideways and turned to the right. The heels should be from 4 inches to 8 inches apart [toes pointing outwards] so that a line from the centre of one target would pass through them to the centre of the other. The body should be upright, head erect, both legs straight, the weight of the body resting principally on the heels, the position being easy and without constraint.
>
> The left hand should then be raised, the arm fully extended, when the first knuckle of the forefinger should line up to the gold. If it does not, it should be brought down. If to the left of the target the toes should be turned very slightly to the right, without moving the heels; the hand should be once more raised and the action repeated as necessary until the gold is covered. If the hand were initially to the right the toes should be moved to the left.

Left, a type of club uniform dress for ladies and gentlemen, c. 1860, from *The Archer's Guide*. Note the gentleman's high draw. Right, Col. H. Walrond demonstrating his careful style. (*Author*)

When the proper position has been found the shoulders will be at right angles to the target. The angle at which the feet are and the position of the toes should be carefully noted and remembered and never deviated from. It is absolutely necessary that the position of the shoulders be acquired in this way and not by turning the body at the hips, for if this is done the body will inevitably twist back at the loose. The proper stance should be obtained thus for every end and when secured the feet should not move until three arrows have been loosed.

The Edwardian period saw some of the best scores made in competitive archery and it is sad that so many of the young men who had benefited from his knowledge should perish a decade later in the trenches.

We have so far looked at British and European attitudes to the importance of posture and stance. It is time now to move further afield and to the United States.

Recreational archery in the United States might be said to have begun on September 26, 1828, when five young friends formed themselves into the United Bowmen of Philadelphia[16] and held a meeting for target practice. The length shot was just fifty yards and the results unremarkable but, in 1829, with distance now increased to eighty yards, an inaugural "Annual Prize Meeting" took place when the same five archers again shot. Member Dr. Griffith won with fourteen hits and a score of 62, therefore being declared the first champion archer of the United States. The Round, of eighty-four arrows at eighty yards, shot two way, thus established the oldest traditional American Round.

The May 1878 edition of the popular U.S. magazine *Scribner's Monthly*[17] carried a commentary by Maurice Thompson on American archery in earlier years. He wrote, "until lately, in the United States archery has been confined to here and there. An individual enthusiast or a small family group forming the nucleus of a small club whose targets and shooting has never been seen but by 'familiar friends'." By the 1870s however, many properly constituted societies had been formed and archery was accepted generally as a desirable activity, and no longer seen as a quaint anachronistic pastime.

For readers, Thompson offers a brief account of a day's shooting by his own society. He writes

> In June a merry little company of ladies and gentlemen climbed, with some difficulty on the part of the ladies, into a large farm wagon and trundled off for a day's shooting in a "great and dusky wood." Here in the midst of their chosen ground there was a sweet spring of cool clear water and on the grass beside this targets were erected and shooting commenced.

When this had finished and the addition of scores was taking place it was noticed that one of the ladies was missing; she soon emerged however, quite distressed, from a nearby thicket bearing in one hand her bow, and in the other a dead rabbit, transfixed by her arrow. Thompson records that she, "declared her intention never again to shoot at a living thing." The day concluded with "shooting at 'rovers,' up and back the brooklet's green bank before packing all away and departing for home."

The account is explicit of the pleasure Thompson and his club colleagues derived from archery and no doubt fired readers with the enthusiasm to do likewise.

With archery now nationally recognized, the creation of a National Archery Association was conceived. The enthusiast leading this enterprise, and its first secretary, was Henry C. Carver of the Chicago Archery Association. The first elected president was Maurice Thompson.

The inaugural national event was held in 1879 with eighty-nine archers present, sixty-nine of whom were men, and twenty women.[18] Sadly however, despite the enthusiasm with which the event began, this quickly evaporated and for many years attendance flagged.

The next offer of help for the long-suffering American archer came in the form of advice within *The Archers Complete Guide* by an "Expert,"[19] an advertising booklet from Messrs Peck and Snyder of New York published in 1878. At that time, much archery tackle was being imported from the United Kingdom, and Peck and Snyder were principal importers of bows from the firm of Philip Highfield, London.

The self-styled expert, who does not identify himself, brings little that is new to the scene as far as shooting goes. However, his opening commentary is somewhat reminiscent of the first part of *Toxophilus*, in that he writes at great length of the history of the bow and a number of other facts which he deems of interest; it is not until we reach page eleven that he begins to extol the virtues of archery and lead on to the use of the bow following a long discussion on the equipment. His advice on standing is sound however.

> The archer being in front of the target with the arrow nocked, the next step is to take his standing. This attitude is graceful and gives perfect control of the muscles. The body must be at right angles to the target, the left side being exact-

ly opposed to it, with the face turned over the left shoulder and squarely facing the target. Let the feet be flat on the ground, the heels six inches apart, the toe of the left foot advanced towards the mark, the form erect, with the bust [sic] fully expanded and the head a little forward.

Illustrative drawing of the "correct attitude" from *The Archers Complete Guide.* Note that the artist appears to have shown the archer using just one finger to draw back the string. (*Author*)

He does not confine himself to advice on shooting, he is also concerned with its physical value. "As a bodily exercise archery may be described as walking, lifting, thrusting, leaping, boxing, and fencing all in one, with the most violent and objectionable of each left out."

He is lyrical: "From the soles of his feet to the crown of his head the archer feels every physical power spring into action."

He turns to the lady archer:

> If proper attention is not neglected, the most delicate lady, not an invalid, may practice archery in the open air with impunity, so that it not be raining. Those who have no experience in the matter will perhaps be slow to believe that in three short months, a most fragile young woman, by means of judicious archery practice, developed muscles that when her arms were flexed, rolled up into balls like a blacksmith's biceps.

Whether the thought of acquiring a blacksmith's biceps actually appealed to genteel ladies of the leisured class we may doubt, but perhaps they accepted the general purpose of his advice.

Our expert is also concerned about preparation for the activity:

> It should not be indulged immoderately after eating, or sleeping. Nor should one go at once from close exhaustive

mental work to shooting with a bow. An hour's quiet after eating, and a half hour's leisurely sauntering in the open air on quitting brain labour will suffice in this regard.

Of smoking he says disapprovingly, "If a gentleman must smoke let it be after the shooting is over," while the ladies are equally admonished. "A lady who wears a tight corset need not hope for much benefit from archery, or for that matter from anything else!" A man with forthright views and not averse to sharing them.

The final source to be examined is the *Spencer System of Shooting the Bow*[20] containing advice for American archers contributed by national champion Stanley Spencer.

Spencer was virtually self-taught. A powerfully built man, he was essentially a bow hunter whose early shooting experience was with legendary bow hunter Will Compton, his friend and mentor. An association that he said influenced his casual and relaxed style.

Spencer's first venture into the cut and thrust of true competitive archery was at the 1926 National Archery Association's Championships in Philadelphia which he won. He was convinced that this success was due to his relaxed style, and his book, published in 1933, offers this system to the archery population at large. His book is a detailed and nicely presented account of his study of "relaxed" shooting and its associated principles together with advice on the development of a system for its practice. We will see what he has to say.

Spencer does not dwell overly on foot position, reflecting only that it should feel "comfortable, well-balanced and braced," with weight distributed evenly on both feet. His advice resulting from years of successful competitive archery is to stand naturally straight—not the forced straightness as when shooting with a gun, but as if one were at ease with something familiar.

He is concerned with the head position, advising that it be turned, "so that the target is fully visible without moving your body or rolling your eyes. . . . The left arm should hang loosely with the bow in the left hand."

There is little doubt that Spencer was a successful archer. He won other tournaments—although not again nationally, never being as he says, "at the right place at the right time." As others have done after him, he capitalized on his success, and his enthusiasm for his system was no doubt a source of encouragement to other pre-war American target archers.

Position of head and hand as illustrated in the *Spencer System of Shooting the Bow*. Note good, straight back of the hand and slightly side of the face draw, with hand below chin. (*Author*)

It is interesting to note that no expert, not even Horace Ford, distinguishes the stance appropriate to clout or distance shooting, from that for target or butt. In Ford's case that might be expected since clout shooting was then almost entirely confined to the Warwickshire society, the Woodmen of Arden. It was however a feature, although a small one of Edwardian archery, and as such Colonel Walrond might have been expected to comment. By 1926, American archers were fully familiar with this aspect of their sport, but were offered no shooting advice by specialist Stanley Spencer.

In the first two chapters we have looked at the varied views of knowledgeable pundits both medieval and modern across the centuries and noted their individual solutions for perfect position and stance. In the next two we will take matters further and look to these experts for their advice on the holding, nocking, and drawing of the longbow, together with the aim and loose.

THREE

Holding the Bow, Nocking, and Drawing

"Drawing well is the best part of shootinge. . . . Holdinge must not be longe for it both putteth a bowe in jeopardy and also marreth a man's shot."—Roger Ascham, *Toxophilus*

With varied and sometimes contradictory advice on the correct position and stance behind us, it is time to look at the next stage in preparation for the shot; the correct way to hold the bow, the nocking—placing the arrow on the string, and the drawing up of the longbow as perceived by our various experts. We will start by turning once more to the author of that late fifteenth century *L'art d' Archerie* for his advice. For this we will examine the ninth chapter of his manuscript, that which is headed "The Shooting with a Bow."[1]

He opens by telling the archer, "first to poise his bow on the thumb of the hand in which he holds it when he shoots"—an enigmatic comment which suggests perhaps that, unusually, left handed archers may have been tolerated in France during those far off days. He continues, "for butt shooting he should balance it exactly"—advice which indicates a different hand position for other styles of shooting, and which is particularly interesting as it seems to tell us how all archers in earlier days may have held their bows. He adds, "If the bow is well made the upper limb will be the longest." As we shall later see, once the position is established another early writer mentions the practice of smearing this with beeswax to help with finding it again.

Continuing the instruction, "He should draw an arrow from his quiver in two motions, the reason being that unless he has a very long arm, the arrow would remain jammed in the quiver." (French arrows of that period were at least "ten palms breadths" long, so taking a palm's breadth as a nominal 3 1/2 inches this would suggest an arrow of 35 inches in length.)

> Then, holding the arrow by its middle he must put it in the bow [nock it] and then hold it between two fingers, the first and second.
>
> And every good archer should draw his bow with three fingers and to his right breast so he can pull a longer arrow. As to drawing, it can be done in two ways; some draw with the bow hand raised, and some with it low down and each is good in different ways. The string should be held on the second joint of the first finger, and on the first joint of the third.

Curiously, this hold, which is unusual and counter to modern practice, was still recommended by a modern French archery coach.[2]

Our medieval instructor concludes, "Drawing with the bow hand low is good for butt and target shooting than with the bow hand high, besides which it assists the loose." This seems to suggest something similar to the "V" draw—lifting both arms to full draw at the same time—and the "T" draw—presenting the bow arm towards the target, then completing the draw with the drawing arm—methods which will be understood by traditional archers of today.

We know a little of the equipment used in France and England during those far off days. Bows were of two section shapes, either "square" or "round." The square, we are told, was best for butt shooting, while the round for target and flight shooting. Those for target shooting had a broader back, while for flight shooting backs were narrower. Horn tips (stringing horns) are mentioned— malleable cow horn for target bows and the harder stag horn for flight—to add elasticity to the bow limbs.

Of bow strings we learn that raw green silk made the best for flight shooting since the elasticity of silk was said to add impetus to the shot. Hemp, which as we know was also used, was always to be obtained from the female plant.

Arrows for butt and target shooting were best made from aspen (poplar), well seasoned for a year or two without artificial heat, while for flight shooting the stiffer birch wood was desirable.

Fletchings of medieval French arrows were either glued or bound into position with waxed silk, the latter method seeming to have been preferred. Of the glued arrows there were two sorts: sheaf and flight. The sheaf arrow was usually thick, with large high cut swan feathers and iron heads—said to have been as used by the English for butt and target shooting. Flight arrows were of light but stiff wood, although our French author acknowledges, "they are not as good as English examples."

He advises that each flight arrow be fletched with three pigeon or duck feathers, each fletch three "small fingers" long. Heads should be of horn or iron. Shafts could be either solid or hollow. Hollow shafts were bored to just below the shaftment (the area where the feathers lay) and the hole filled with lead or mercury. These hollow shafts were considered dishonorable however, for the advantage they gave could not be seen; solid arrows, we are told, were the more honest with which to shoot.

We will return later to our medieval archer to learn more of his fifteenth century advice, but now we will move forward sixty years to toxophilite Roger Ascham who has many positive things to say about nocking the shaft and holding it and says them in his forthright, no nonsense way.

> To nock well is the easiest thing of all, and there is no cunning, but only a diligent heed giving not to set the shaft too high or too low, but ever straight and athwart his bow for inconstant nocking makes a man lose his length.

This throws an interesting light on Tudor archery. Today we whip or "serve" our bow strings as a matter of course, and include both a "nocking point" for surety of arrow positioning, and an arrow pass just above the bow handle to indicate the hand position. It seems that perhaps this was not then practice, since Ascham goes on to say that, "if the shaft hand is high and the bow hand is low, or the contrary, then the bow is in danger of breaking."

"Drawing well," he continues, "is the best part of shooting. Men in old times used another method of shooting than we now do. They used to draw low at the breast, to the right pap and no further. Nowadays we draw to the right ear and not to the pap." He is of course speaking of English archery, but one wonders how aware he was of French practice a mere fifty years earlier, and the advice of our anonymous French writer to "draw it to his right breast."

In passing, it is interesting to find a reference in the earliest of the folk tales of our English hero Robin Hood, dating perhaps to the fourteenth century if not earlier, where, at an archery tournament the Sheriff of Nottingham exhorts Robin to "draw it [the bow] to thine ear."[3] If these tales are as early as some scholars believe, then perhaps the common practice, yet to be changed, was to hold and draw to the chest, a style common in England since Saxon times. However, Robin was an excellent archer, if we are to believe the ballads, and probably needed no reminding.

Ascham has advice for drawing the bow. "If shooting at pricks [target], hasty and quick drawing is neither sure nor comely. Therefore to draw easily and uniformly—that is to say not wagging your hand upward or downward but always in one fashion until you reach the ridge or shoulder of your [arrow] head is best for profit and seemliness." (Tudor target arrowheads were shouldered in two ways as a check on draw-length, either by "ridging" or by creating a "silver spoon" style—so named from its resemblance to a contemporary sixteenth-century spoon.) "Holding must not be long for it both puts the bow in jeopardy and also spoils a man's shot. It should be so little that it may be perceived better in a man's mind when it is done than seen with a man's eyes when it is in the doing." Wise advice that resonates with coaches today.

We have already noticed from *l'Art d'Archerie* that men poised their bows on their thumbs to find the point of balance. Ascham adds to this: "fine wax shall do very well to show where a man holds his bow." He then defines the style of drawing in the sixteenth century, a style with variants recommended by later writers which we will notice below. "When a man shooteth, the might of his shoot lieth upon the foremost finger and on the ring [third] finger, for the middle finger which is the longest bears no weight of the string at all." This is a strange comment, since we believe that archers of earlier times shot with just two fingers on the string, the forefinger and the middle finger.

Holding the shaft to the string too hard rubs the skin from the fingers he says, and to keep them apart he advises sewing a split goose quill to the fingers of the glove—modern archers use a spacer on their leather tabs for a similar purpose.

Holding the arrow on the string preparatory to shooting is of course dependent upon the arrow nock or string groove. In modern arrows these nocks are bell-shaped to allow the arrow to be held firmly but lightly, independent of the fingers and thus without the need for pinching. In Ascham's day nock designers had yet to adopt this feature. String grooves then came in various styles, each with its virtue and its problem. He lists them: "some great and full, some handsome and small, some round, and some long, some wide and some narrow, some deep and some shallow. Some with one nock and some with a double nock for "the double surety of the shaft."

This reference to double nocking provokes some questions since the meaning is not at all clear. Does "surety" here mean safety, or does it mean convenience. It is possible that the slit cut diagonally across the string nock to take the horn insert was called double nocking; many arrows in a fifteenth-century inventory are said to be "cross-nocked," while within a later seventeenth century work there is a reference to "cross-slitting" which in the context seems to mean the insertion of a horn nock-piece. The references are enigmatic and need explanation.

Although many of the arrows recovered from the Tudor warship *Mary Rose* are cross-slitted to take a nock piece, there is no evidence of a second diagonal string nock. Equally however, a second arrow nock at right angles is used in modern times by those who shoot for speed. The jury is out on this one.

Our next expert, Gervase Markham, copies Ascham almost to the letter; we can therefore disregard him and move forward a century again to Thomas Roberts and his 1801 work, *The English Bowman*.[4]

Roberts mentions the eighteenth-century practice, which seems to have been newly (re)introduced of preventing irregular nocking by whipping (we would say, serving) the exact nocking-point on the string with silk of one color, while whipping on either side with silk of a different color, to the breadth of the drawing fingers. He warns that if the arrow is to fly "true to the mark," care should be taken that the nocking point itself should not fit the shaft so tightly that it might burst the arrow nock itself. The nock then was bell-shaped to hold the shaft securely on the string, removing the need for it to be squeezed between the fingers. This may perhaps have been a comparatively recent innovation—two well made mid-eighteenth century arrows in my possession are without this feature. Roberts draws attention to the "little click" as the string enters the "bell" and remarks that the arrow cannot fall from it. Without the need to squeeze the arrow to keep it on the string, the loose was evidently cleaner and therefore contributed to a more accurate shot.

Once it was on the string, Roberts comments that the arrow should rest between the bow and the first joint of the first finger, pressing against the bow. He suggests that the finger might be raised a little to make a better "socket or groove" for the arrow to lie in, while the end joint of the finger should be bent a little inwards.

In the matter of drawing the bow, Roberts has this to say. "There is some difference among archers in the mode of drawing. Some extend their arm completely before they begin to draw which certainly is the easiest method (today we would call this the "T draw") others extend it gradually as they draw."

In a penciled note within his own copy of the book he has written rather more explicitly.

An engraving used by Thomas Roberts in his book as an example of good style. It is thought to be Sir Ashton Lever. *(Author)*

> Drawing. Strongly but gently and evenly to ear without turning or drawing the string out of its line. Cross the Mark perpendicularly with the point of the arrow, taking aim over the forefinger, which raise to the Mark. Bow hand wrist being sufficiently elevated, and keep eye fixed on the centre of the mark against a wind, when the aim, must be above the Mark. Draw bow far back beyond the body, stiffening the drawing arm to give support.[5]

Ascham has remarked that in his time some very good archers drew their arrows to within two inches of the pile, paused for a moment and having corrected their aim, drew fully home and loosed, but this method he faults, insisting that drawing and loosing should be one continuous movement.

Taking up Ascham's point, Roberts comments that several of the best archers of his day (late eighteenth century) "both practise, and approve of, this fault. Other good archers draw within two inches of the pile, then draw and re-draw within these two inches until they loose." Roberts calls this "playing with and humouring" the bow.

Archers of Thomas Waring's time in three poses: stringing the bow, waiting his turn, and shooting. (*Author*)

He comments then upon the position in which the bow is held when drawing the string, noting that most prints of old-time archers invariably show them holding their bows vertically. However, he remarks that several of the best archers of his day "hold their bows somewhat obliquely." Noting this he observes however that, "the more distant the mark, the more perpendicularly must the bow be held."

Digging now deeper into the nineteenth century, we turn once more to bowyer Thomas Waring the Younger and his 1814 *Treatise of Archery*. This young man aged just seventeen, had successfully taken charge of his father's established bow-making business and was now, as a twenty-six-year-old adult, about to display an independent and questioning mind uninfluenced by contemporary practice.

About the holding of the bow, he writes, "The top of the handle must be level with the top of the hand, for as the resistance

from each end is where the bow is held, so, if the hand is shift-
ed the centre of action is changed accordingly." No problem
with this comment of course, but then he continues:

> The left arm which holds the bow must be held out quite
> straight—the surest way to do this will be to turn the wrist in
> as much as possible, as by this means the bow being grasped
> only very easily, will rest firm in the hand; but if the arm is not
> turned in, the strength of the bow will fall upon the thumb,
> and as a consequence of such holding it can never be drawn
> up to the head of the arrow.

He carries on with this curious and rather controversial
advice. "Remember then that the arm will be so turned in that
the string strikes it when released. The blow will hurt the arm
without some protection, but that will be treated of hereafter."

Protection was through the wearing of a bracer or arm-guard.
The author possesses a lady's arm-guard of this period with
telling evidence of the continued striking of a bow string. We
will be treated to champion archer Horace Ford's view of this
odd arrangement later.

Waring concludes: "When drawing the bow let the whole of
the hand rest upon the handle, yet let the part between the
thumb and finger feel the most pressure."

We will meet young Thomas Waring again in a later chapter
where he presents mathematical logic for the revision of the values of scoring rings on targets. But in the meantime let us move
more deeply into the nineteenth century and to the thoughts of
bow and arrow maker, and practicing bowman, Hezekiah Dixon.
His advice was made available to the questing archer when, in
1855, the archery firm of A.N. Myers produced a small handbook written by Dixon.[6]

Although based largely on Thomas Waring's earlier *Treatise*,
with some additional comment, the preamble to this booklet is
interesting as a philosophical commentary upon attitudes to their
young by those of the leisured social class who had adopted
archery as a pastime.

Our present system of keeping children in warm rooms for the greater part of their infant existence instead of letting them live chiefly in the open air, and become hardened to the varying influences, is a certain means of bringing up delicate young ladies and gentlemen, in the place of a hardy race of boys and girls which once existed

The healthful nature of the exercise is indisputable, and the graceful action of the limbs which it encourages may well make it a favoured exercise with those who desire the best development of the human figure. The early and constant practice of archery, and suchlike arts would prevent many a distortion of the figure in young females which cause anxiety to parents and lead to the necessity for reclining boards, artificial supports and all that array of apparatus so painfully familiar to invalids.

He adds, "The evil is so great especially in the neighbourhood of towns that we cannot too strongly enforce the necessity for amusements which shall bring out our young folk into the gardens and the fields, and keep them employed there for hours, that they may breathe fresh air and experience the wholesome influences of country and suburb and," he ends, "what more elegant than archery?"

The homily over, he passes on some helpful hints.

When drawing up the bow he advises the shooter to

look a little to the left of the knuckles, not along the arrow; the bow must not be held so as to bring the pile of the arrow in a line with the eye and the hand for if it is, the arrow when shot will go considerably to the left of the mark. During this, the bow may be held quite straight with the string upwards. The string should be held nearly up to the first joint of the finger.

Waring's controversial advice to strike the bracer when shooting is omitted, as are other contentious aspects of his *Treatise*.

Dixon also advises that the bow should not be "elevated" while partially drawn, for in reaching for the string, the right hand he says, "alters the position of the bow."

Wise, if rather wordy, and somewhat woolly advice is given about drawing up the bow without an arrow including:

> On no account ought a gentleman take up a lady's bow, even with its proper arrows. For his strength being greater he may draw it beyond the power of the bow.
>
> Never draw up any bow, even in a room, without a proper arrow within it. Many intending only to try its strength do not think this precaution necessary, and draw it too far. An arrow is a guide and warns when to stop.
>
> Never draw a bow when someone is standing before you, for they might be injured if the bow broke.

With Hezekiah and his helpful hints for parents behind us, let us now move further still into the nineteenth century and to the firm of Thomas Aldred who, on the basis of the number of his bows known to have survived, must have been one of the most prolific of the nineteenth-century makers of archery tackle.

Close association with archery brought with it a deep interest in the pastime and, in 1854, although by then still not fully committed to the business of making bows, as we have earlier seen, he invited a noted archer, the Reverend Francis Merewether, to prepare a booklet, *The Young Archer's Assistant*. In this, although little is actually said of the draw, a subject of this chapter, Merewether writes eloquently of the physical value of archery.

> There is no great difficulty in perceiving how archery operates so wonderfully as a healthy amusement; for in shooting, nearly every muscle in the body is brought into action, and the expansion of the chest in particular is one of many benefits resulting from it. Very considerable exercise is also unsuspectingly gained and this too, in the open air. And it is by no means the least of the recommendations of archery that ladies can take part in it without imputation of being thought masculine, or of taking part in an amusement which some consider to be solely confined to the other sex.

This comment is interesting since it reflects the change in social attitude towards women that had taken place since the preceding century; we may note here that in the Royal British Bowmen seventy years earlier, women shared full equality of membership with men.

Merewether is one of the few writing on archery practice who comments upon clothing.

> We cannot too strongly urge the necessity of the dress, both for ladies and gentlemen, being as loose and easy as possible, as any tightness prevents the free action of the arms and consequently increases the difficulty of shooting in proper manner.
>
> Gentlemen who wear rings are recommended to remove them from their left hand at all events; and a cap will be found much more convenient to shoot in than a hat. [The top hat was standard wear for many men at that time.]

He treads warily though on the matter of women's headgear: "The present fashion of ladies bonnets has this recommendation; viz. That they are not so much in the way of the string as they used to be." The later Victorian fashion of hats abundantly decorated with floral displays had yet to appear on target lines.

Although Aldred (or Merewether) aimed his advice towards the young, he offered much that was relevant to the adult archer.

Of those who have written with authority on shooting the longbow, national champion archer Horace Ford leads the field. As we have already seen, in 1859 he produced his seminal work *Archery: Its Theory and Practice* and it was an instant success. He was acknowledged by all as an outstanding archer, and although there may have been those who eyed his practice scores with suspicion[7] no one could doubt those he made while competing nationally.

His views on holding the bow were well thought through and his advice was relevant. He believed that the most natural and easy position was the best, adding that this applied equally to almost everything connected with archery; here Roger Ascham's insistence upon "comliness" is recalled.

He takes issue with Thomas Waring's advice to "turn the wrist in as much as possible," remarking that the

> left arm will then be held in such a position that it would be a constant obstacle to the free passage of the string, causing it to hit the bracer or the unprotected arm, and the cause of an increased strain and additional effort to the shooter, besides affecting the natural 'spring' of the wrist and arm.
>
> Conversely, if the wrist is intentionally turned outward, as some do [Ford mentions the tendency of women to do this] then the whole force of the bow is upon it and it becomes unequal to the task.

As Ford remarks, "extremes are bad in every instance and to be avoided." His advice, when the arrow is nocked, is to "let the bow lie easily and lightly in the left hand, with the wrist turned neither inward nor outward, but allowed to remain in the position nature intended, for as the bow is drawn, the position of the hand and wrist will be easiest for the archer and best for a successful shot."

Ford goes on to discuss the position of the thumb of the left hand, noting that some archers extend it along the belly of the bow. He mentions also that some extend their fore finger to keep the arrow in place. Each of these habits is bad says Ford, since they tend to weaken the grasp.

He also discusses the position of the bow when being drawn. "Whether it should be held horizontally, or obliquely (canted at a slight angle) opinions amongst archers are equally divided, with the majority favouring the canted position."

After considering the matter, Ford recommends canting the bow slightly, since it assumes that position naturally in the hand when being drawn. An additional advantage is the help the position gives in a side wind. A third reason is that it slightly bends the elbow naturally, helping to keep the arm away from the passage of the string.

Ford devotes a full twelve-page chapter to drawing the bow, and in doing so he reveals much about the practice of his contemporaries. Today we are accustomed to coming to full draw and holding that position until release; it was seemingly not always so. Ford instances archers who varied the length of their draw when shooting at various distances—a shorter draw for shorter distances, while for longer distances raising or lowering the drawing hand. As he remarks, it is the bow hand that should be raised or lowered. Advice in contradiction to modern ideas of a straight "draw force line"—of which more later.

Horace Ford demonstrates his easy, "natural poise." (*Author*)

He then turns to the bow arm and the instruction by some experts to hold it "as straight as possible." He rounds particularly on Thomas Waring and the advice in his Treatise on Archery which advises that the left hand be "so turned that the string strike it when loosed." Ford suggests sarcastically that "had he [Waring] directed the shooter to stand on his head when drawing his bow, or closing his eyes when aiming, it had hardly been the more injurious doctrine."

Ford closes his lengthy chapter on the draw by commenting again upon the practice of many men who still drew to the breast, "a bad method, indeed the very worst, as it circumscribes the pull, most materially diminishes the archer's power over the bow and causes the line of sight to be so much above the arrow that the difficulty of setting aim (as regards elevation) at the shorter distances is very great indeed."

Moreover, he concludes, when shot in this way the arrow flies as if it is "sent from a broomstick rather than from a bow; for the archer's position is so cramped and huddled that he not only loses much of his natural poise, but also that thorough command of the string necessary for a good loose." The writer recalls a highly respected archery colleague of advanced years who drew low because, as he said, nature refused to let him bend.

Summarizing, Ford stresses the need for the draw to be even, quiet and steady, without jerk or sudden involuntary movement. To do otherwise can result in damage to the bow through crysalling (belly compression fracturing), besides disturbing the flight of the arrow.

We shall meet Ford again when we move to the acts of aiming, releasing, and following through.

Ford's book remained the *vade mecum* for many nineteenth-century archers familiar with his style and results. By the turn of the twentieth century however they were either gone or in their dotage and it was time for a re-statement of shooting advice.

We have already met with Colonel Walrond's 1904 booklet, *Archery for Beginners* and noticed his advice for the stance. It is now time to look at his thoughts on holding and drawing up the bow.

By the beginning of the twentieth century, largely through trial and error and despite the advice of self-styled experts, many of the principles of good archery had been assimilated and now formed part of main-stream practice. The mechanics involved in drawing the bow were more fully understood and these, with the associated loose and follow-through, contributed to the record York and National Rounds then shot.

Describing the act of drawing, Walrond advises

> Raise the hands simultaneously until the first finger of the left hand is on the gold (the grasp on the bow gradually tightening as it comes up), and the forefinger of the right hand is just below the chin and touching it, the right elbow being rather

above the level of the shoulder without in any way moving head or body. During these motions the right hand should move close to the body, the elbow being kept well to the rear and not moving out from the body, keeping the little finger of the right hand slightly extended and letting it touch the body as the hand comes up will be found a help in securing the correct movement. [He continues] It is most important that the head should be kept quite still, the right hand being brought to the chin and not the chin to the hand. [Today we call moving the face towards the string rather than the other way around "loading the head."] Care must also be taken not to overdraw the arrow.

The left arm will now be fully extended with the right hand just under the chin, the forearm nearly in line with the arrow, the elbow slightly raised [we would call this the "draw force-line"] and well to the rear.

The arrow is now ready to be aimed.

We will meet with more of this forthright commentary later and move now to the last of those giving freely of their knowledge.

Although Walrond's booklet is perhaps the last to give detailed advice specific to shooting the longbow for British archers, the book produced by Stanley Spencer in 1926 and mentioned in an earlier chapter provided a similar service to his American colleagues. We will dip once more into this to study his self-proclaimed system for holding and drawing the bow.

Continuing his theme of the relaxed approach Spencer advises letting the hand hang naturally when taking up the bow.

Then without twisting it, raise your arm straight out from your side to a level with your shoulder, noticing that the hand is about level with it across the back. Then tip the hand straight back at the wrist and leave the thumb out from the hand slightly and mark this position well. Then put the bow on the thumb and tilt the tip to about 10 degrees to the right, having your drawing fingers on the string to hold the bow in position.

This would seem to mean, place the bow in the yoke of the thumb and forefinger. He then adds

> Leave the left hand open and relaxed. Draw the bow up a few times to allow it to find its resting position; you will soon find that it "rides" perfectly.
>
> You will notice that a bow placed in this way will remain in position as the hand is swung straight out for shooting. You will also notice, in hanging naturally at the side, that the hand is not parallel with the body but that the back of the hand is turned forward quite a bit and the bow when in place at your side will point at about 20 degrees to the left. This leaves it to cross the hand at an angle that places it altogether at the base of the thumb and clear of the rest of the hand.

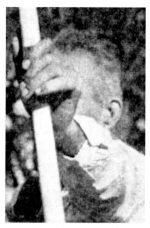

Bow hand position advocated by Stanley Spencer. (*Author*)

Spencer's advice concerning the relaxed position continues in this vein, ending by offering it as an advantage to those who are double jointed, including he says,

> women, since it keeps the arm clear of the string. By placing the bow on the thumb side of the hand, and the hand is at 45 degrees to the horizontal [a position advocated today], the lower part of the arm is kept well back and the thumb is kept clear of the string.
>
> If the arm is locked firm when the string is released the whole body will be jarred and the arrow will jerk either to one side, or up or down. The result is a 'dead arm' that adversely affects arrow flight.

Stanley Spencer is chronologically the last of the experts on shooting the longbow from whose knowledge we may draw, for by 1926 the old weapon was about to run its course, superseded by advances in metallurgy, and the new steel bows.[8]

But now with a surfeit of informed advice from which to draw, we will move to the next chapter, there to study varied views on the aim, the release, and of course, the follow through.

FOUR

The Aim, the Sight, and the Loose

"Lowsinge [Loosing] *must be . . . . So quicke and harde, that it be without girdes* [twitches] *so soft and gentle that the shafte fly not as it were from a bow-case. The meane betwixt both which is perfite lowsinge."*—Roger Ascham, *Toxophilus*

Having settled style and posture, together with draw and hold, to the satisfaction of our various experts, we must now look at the reason for it all. The accurate launch of our arrow in the direction of the mark, hopefully to hit it. But, before tangling with the detail of this we should recognize the subtle distinction between aiming and sighting, for the two are not synonymous. To aim an arrow is to direct its point at the target (*point blanc*) or at a position that will result in a hit. To sight is to use an artificial aid associated with the bow which, being aligned with the target, will similarly achieve this. It is an aid to aiming.

Having noted this distinction, now to the detail. We have looked earlier at the practice of the fifteenth century French archer and noticed an interesting if rather dynamic approach to the essential preliminaries. The very nature of these gyrations would preclude any accurate aiming and we may fairly assume that for short distances they were inappropriate. Unfortunately our anonymous French informant does not mention target shooting and we thus have no guidance to show how *tir a berceau,* the French equivalent of our target archery, was performed.

We will leave the Frenchman to his archery and turn once more to England and the sixteenth century. Matters progress a little here, for Roger Ascham touches on the subject in *Toxophilus.* As he stresses however, intimately connected with aiming is of course the loose and this he describes as ideally "quick and hard," and yet "soft and gentle;" contrasting concepts upon which he does not elaborate, being at pains to say that the perfect loose is as hard to teach as it is to describe. As an aside, the writer recalls the description of a loose by a practitioner of Japanese archery. The loose he said, should be as "snow sliding from a leaf."[1]

Ascham is clear however about the need for there to be no obstruction to the aim and the loose, instancing an ancient emperor who required his archers to be both beardless and bald to avoid entanglement with the bow string, a circumstance which will resonate with some hairy archers of today.

Of aiming itself he has little to say. He writes at a time when marks were more distant than today and he is concerned primarily with the effect of wind and weather on the flight of a shaft and the need to "keep a length."

Rather grudgingly however, it seems he admits that there is one thing that many archers do "that shall cause less need to mark the weather, and that is giving Aim." He is rather at a loss though as to know what to say about this. Clearly he does not approve, although he concedes that in strange places it is helpful, "which is the only praise of it," while adding cautionary advice that wind and weather may change and so affect the shot. He sees every shot being made with due consideration for wind and weather, and for accurate distance shooting he is of course right. "Ame gyvyng" as he calls it, or as we would say today taking (giving) aim he suggests comes with experience gained through long practice since childhood.

He does expand a little further on giving aim, however, observing that to shoot straight men have invented certain different ways, such as noting a tree, or a hill behind the mark. Warming to the subject he instances a man he once saw who laid his gear between the pricks (marks). Some thought he did it for reasons of safety, but Ascham supposes that he did it to provide what today we would call a "point of aim" or as he says "to shoot straight withal."

He concludes by mentioning that other men use a mark of some sort to aim at which is a bow's width from the prick, and of this he appears to approve. An early acceptance of the "archer's paradox" caused by the flexing of the arrow around the bow, if not as yet a full understanding of the cause.

Of all these aids, however he stresses one fundamental thing—having a man's eye always on his mark is the only way to shoot straight, adding that some men when drawing look at their mark until almost at full draw, then look at their shaft, yet at the very instant of loosing find their mark again. He summarizes, "hold and nock truly, draw and loose equally and keep your compass certainly."

His final advice, and that which has been echoed in later times is to take a bow at night and shoot both up and down the field at two lights, for then "a man shall be compelled to look always at the Mark and not at the shaft."

Although there is enough circumstantial evidence from incidents in battle to indicate accuracy at short distance, and this implies practice at pricks, sixteenth-century archers were required by statute to shoot for distance; and butt shooting was conducted at eleven score yards. Events were regularly held in London, when money prizes and silver or gold arrows were awarded for distances shot. If he were present, we can perhaps imagine Roger Ascham as a young man, standing on the sidelines keenly observing stance and mentally noting draw and loose as archers strained and struggled to achieve that elusive prize and the prestige that accompanied it.

These events took place on Finsbury Fields, and among the first recorded may have been that which was held there in 1521.[2] An account of the arrangements survives and these will surely resonate with any modern organizer responsible for a large scale bow meeting. Two important aspects are covered, crowd control and safety. Those responsible for spectators at certain UK football matches today will nod with appreciation at the first.

It was required that, "any man reparyng to [attending] this Game of Shotyng keepe the Kyngs pece [peace] in his owne persone upon the payne of Imprisonment and further to make fyne [be fined] by discretion of the Lord and Maisters present."

Thought was also given to the safety of onlookers whose propensity for getting in the way was no less then than it is today. So they were informed

> No personne approache or cume so nere that he shall stand
> in daunger for his own cause and others. And for the good
> and due orderyng of the same no persone be so hardy [fool-
> ish!] to stande within xx [twenty] yards of any of the stakes
> appoynyted for a mark.

To emphasize this last point a bugle was to be sounded before each shot was made.

Shooting was with three different arrows—standard, bearing, and flight; each archer having a single shot with each. Although there is some dispute concerning the standard arrow, modern consensus seems to suggest that it was an untouched sheaf or "livery" arrow, although whether brought or provided by authority on the day is uncertain. The term bearing is also unclear. A bearing bow is one that shoots true, a personalized weapon perhaps. Thus a bearing arrow is thought to have been a sheaf arrow that had been personally selected, or even personalized to fly true. Each of the standard and bearing shafts would however have carried a war arrowhead. The flight arrow was, and is, a light arrow specifically for distance shooting. What head it carried is uncertain.

Awards for those making the greatest distances with each arrow were considerable for the time.

For the standard arrow, he who "ffayrest [fairest] draweth, clenyest délyvereth and fardest [farthest] of ground shoteth shall have . . . a Crowne of gold of the value of xxs [20 shillings] or xx s in monie therefore."

For the bearing arrow, "an Arowe of gold of the value of xxs or xxs in monie therefore."

For the flight arrow, "a ffly-ght of Golde of the value of xiijs iiijd [13s 4d] in monie therefore."

Artist's impression of a typical parade of archers to the shooting ground. (*Author*)

In addition a reward of 20 pence was given for anyone who exceeded 24 score yards (480 yards) 12 pence for shots in excess of 22 score yards (440 yards) and 8 pence for anything over 20 score yards (400 yards). This bounty may not have continued in future years.

Interest in archery was maintained during most of the sixteenth century, and those concerned with making bows and arrows were kept well occupied. Apprentices were encouraged to join quasi-military archery and handgun groups, headed probably by leaders of the City of London's trained bands who assumed identifying titles. We have noticed one such group, Prince Arthur and his knights, and there were a number of others including a mysterious "Black Train," led by the so far unidentified "Black Prince of Portugal."

An important procession of these groups, together with a full turn-out of city dignitaries, took place in 1583 and is reported to have included 3,000 archers, culminating in an archery event on Hoxton fields.[3] The butt was placed at 148 yards—an unusual shooting distance which may have been that which was safely available at the time or alternatively a distance unfamiliar to those shooting, in order to add a deliberate element of chance.

The shooting took two days to complete, and the awards were substantial for the time. First prize was 53 shillings and 4 pence. Second prize was 5 nobles (a noble was worth roughly 6s 8d); third, 4 nobles; fourth, 20 shillings; fifth, 10 shillings. Also on offer were five gold bows and five silver arrows presented by Prince Arthur's knights. The affair ended in a sumptuous banquet for the principals, of whom there were seemingly a good many, and at this it is said, food was abundant and wine and other drink flowed freely.

All this jollity and archery practice seems not to have lasted however. As the sixteenth century drew to a close the bow was in steady course of replacement by the handgun, and statutory archery practice had fallen off to the degree that those whose living depended upon the manufacture of bows and arrows were seriously affected. With this in mind a treatise *To proove the necessitie and excellence of the use of archerie*[4] was created by "R.S." on behalf of the affected trades. This drew attention to the general disregard of statutory requirements for archery practice and the consequent effect upon their livelihood. It was addressed to the "Nobilitie and Gentlemen of England" who it was no doubt hoped would cause something practical to be done about it.

Even if they were able, they seem not to have done so, since general use of archery continued to decline; for while there is little doubt that among the population at large many owned bows, as Ascham had observed fifty years before, this did not mean they were used and thus required to be replaced.

As we look elsewhere, however, we will notice the roving marks which proliferated on Finsbury Fields, roving being a popular activity with those who retained interest in the longbow. A series of booklets, dubious in their listing of the marks and particularly in their supposed distances, had been produced during the later years of the sixteenth century, and as we enter the seventeenth we will look in some detail at a more exact successor to these early books. This small volume, *Ayme for Finsbury Archers*, published in 1601 and later revised in 1628, would have been a boon both for those unfamiliar with the marks and shooting procedure and—with its accurate measurement of distances—to those archers who regularly shot.[5]

It begins with a statement of its purpose, being for those "unacquainted with the game" and to avoid "controversie" and "rash and unadvised words to the derogation of God's glory."

The number of marks varied—179 are recorded in 1601, although when next revised in 1628 these had diminished to 163. They were variously sponsored by private individuals, livery companies, inns, and even churches. Distances varied, the shortest being nine score (180) yards and the longest nineteen score (390) yards. These distances were established in 1601 and maintained in 1628.

The marks were placed largely at the field boundaries and not scattered in the fields themselves, thus theoretically lessening risk to the populace at large

The last of the marks from Finsbury Fields, called "Scarlet," standing in the Armoury House, home of the Honorable Artillery Company. (*Author*)

who must have taken their lives in their hands while enjoying a leisurely walk along paths within the fields. The dangers to which they were subjected were manifold and the shout of "fast" (stand-fast or stop moving) must have sounded with alarming frequency throughout the day.

Finsbury Fields shared roving marks with other places within London. St George's Fields and Mile End Fields were well supplied and also well supported. Initially it was (at least nominally) the responsibility of the city to maintain and monitor the marks—although those who sponsored them were naturally interested in their upkeep; latterly the role devolved to the Honourable Artillery Company which substituted stone for wood and used them for target practice.[6]

The earlier formal marks were sometimes elaborate structures of wood surmounted by carvings, others were less formal while still imposing; and there were also temporary creations or even a particular bush in a hedge.

Of the hundreds that once graced the fields, just one now survives, and that a late addition. The mark called "Scarlet" stands four-square in the Headquarters of the Honourable Artillery Company. It was removed from a wall near the Canal Bridge in the New North Road, on July 26, 1881. There is an abiding—but so far, to the writer's knowledge, an unsubstantiated—rumor that many of the rest were broken and used as rubble to fill in a depression at the end of the company's ground.

Although roving was the prime activity on Finsbury Fields there were those for whom target and butt shooting were attractions, and the seventeenth century saw the emergence of the Society of Finsbury Archers purely for that purpose. The exact year is unrecorded; but a reference within the annals of the Honourable Artillery Company for 1623 mentions two stewards of the society and this suggests an earlier origin. Although it seems unlikely that there was any significant activity during the conflict between king and parliament from 1642 until 1651, there is circumstantial evidence for meetings or "feasts" at which stewards were elected. There was evidently a resurgence following peace however, since record shows a gathering in 1652[7] to discuss matters concerned with the "General Society of Archers in and About the City of London." At this it was agreed that money should be levied towards the cost of providing the annual feast when discussion of society matters took place, in order not to overburden the stewards with cash flow problems.

While prick (or butt) shooting at eleven score yards may have happened earlier, 1671 seems to have been the year in which matters were regularized and rules drawn up for its proper ordering.[8] A target had been designed by the society and it was to be at this that shooting would take place. The features of this "targett" are not described, but are thought to have consisted of concentric colored rings, the central one of gold—forerunner of the modern version. The target itself would perhaps have been oilcloth on pasteboard and portable; although it is possible that a straw target had been prepared, since this was the style of that adopted by the Society of Archers at Scorton in 1673. It was to be set upon a stand breast high from the ground. The cost of entry was twenty shillings, of which thirty pence was deducted to provide silver plate for prizes.

Shooting was to begin at 8 o'clock in the morning and to carry on until nightfall. Eleven score (220) yards was the distance for butt practice set down by statute of Henry VIII and was therefore of historical significance. Those taking part in this inaugural shoot numbered thirty-two and five of those shooting were knights. Among these, Sir John Robinson—past Lord Mayor of London and an excellent shot—was a prominent participant.

The Braganza Shield. (*Author*)

An interesting feature of arrangements at that time was the facility for an archer to nominate a "stand-in" to shoot in his place if sickness or business were to keep him away. Whether the stand-in had claim to any subsequent award should he be fortunate enough to win the captain's or lieutenant's prize is unknown to the writer.

The Society of Archers is notable for its inferred connection with King Charles's wife, Queen Catherine of Braganza. In 1676 a splendidly engraved silver breast plate was purchased by subscription and known as the Braganza Shield.[9] It was worn by the society's Marshal (Sir) William Wood when, in that year, he led the society to a meeting at which the queen was present. It is thought that the society hoped for her recognition and perhaps her patronage. Although there is no evidence for either, the society informally adopted the title, "Catherine of Braganza Archers."

While still buoyant and successful for half of the eighteenth century, the loss of shooting ground, and perhaps a lessening of interest among the ageing membership, led to the closure of the society. A last, poorly attended meeting took place in 1761.

Before this however, the death of Cromwell and the rejection of his son and successor in favor of the return of monarchy in

The Scorton silver arrow and associated medals. (*Courtesy of the Society of Archers*)

the person of Charles II in 1660 was the catalyst for a great archery contest in Finsbury Fields on the lines of those arranged in the previous century.[10] Held in 1663 in the presence of the Lord Mayor Sir John Robinson and other dignitaries, both the Society of Finsbury archers and the Honourable Artillery Company were closely involved. The standard arrow, now enigmatically named the "pound" arrow, along with the broad arrow and the flight arrow, were each shot in turn. The award for flight shooting was won by Lawrence Girlington, a prominent member and sometime steward of the Finsbury Archers, with an exceedingly impressive twenty two score (440) yards; for which he received a rather meager 10 shillings. He also won the pound arrow contest (a 13s 4d prize) and came second to a Captain Taylour with the broad arrow (an 8 shillings prize) thus ending the day £1 11s 4d to the good.

Archery among the leisured class diminished after the death of King Charles in 1685, since his successor took no great interest in the activity. The pastime still survived however, both in London and in the provinces. Thus, a number of gentlemen archers who had met at Scorton in Yorkshire in 1673 to shoot annually for a silver arrow persevered, and their meeting is still celebrated annually to this day.

There are two enigmas associated with this long-lived meeting. The rules, which are explicit, show significant similarity with those of the Finsbury Society, and although one is not acknowledged, are suggestive of a connection. The silver arrow itself is also enigmatic; it consists of two joined parts and its origin is speculative. If however the Scorton Society Rules were associated initially with those of Finsbury perhaps the (broken) arrow had a similar association. The arrow was given by the Wastell family of Scorton on the understanding that its origin should not be disclosed. A certain John Wastell was a member of the Honourable Artillery Company with which the Finsbury Archers were closely connected; and in 1654 a silver arrow was lost. Was there a connection? The thought is intriguing but we shall never know. [11]

As we have already noticed it was not until the last quarter of the eighteenth century that archery as a social recreation came once more to prominence among the leisured upper class. One of the more important of the societies formed at that time was the Royal British Bowmen, briefly mentioned in an earlier chapter.[12] The society was formed in 1787 and was chief among those few groups that admitted women as equal shooting members. As with its contemporaries, much attention was paid to social activity, with festive fare and dancing taking equal place with shooting.

A record of the conduct of the meetings has been briefly mentioned in an earlier chapter. The ethos of the society at least in its earlier days was to create a sort of rural atmosphere, or to be more exact a sanitized version of one. Thus, all had to leave their expensive courtly gowns and elaborate hairstyles and make-up behind, and appear as rosy cheeked country maidens, dressed in "stuff," a kind of coarse linen. This was not to the liking of all ladies, particularly the more mature. There was fortunately a rule which allowed ladies of sixty years and beyond to dress normally; it would seem that most unusually for the female sex, there were those ladies who claimed to be older than they actually were.

After shooting, and a meal of bacon and beans—supposed country fare—simplicity and shooting costumes were discarded for more elaborate dress of the ballroom, and an evening of lively dancing began.

With simplicity went moral rectitude; for among the rules was one which banned gambling while shooting was in progress. Any such discovered was forfeit to the Society. Members were reproved, "The exercise of archery is to provide amusement, not promote gambling."

Leaving these earlier centuries we will turn once more to Thomas Roberts to check his comments about archery, and specifically the loose of two hundred years ago. He restates the view that it is the most difficult of all the aspects of shooting and the one that must be studied and practiced assiduously. He sees the need to keep the bow arm very firm at the moment of releasing the string, a vice-like grip upon which he says the steady flight of the arrow depends. He advocates bringing the elbow of the drawing arm round and releasing whilst drawing with no pause before the loose. This dynamic release has its problems however, since there is much scope for variation, with no positive draw check, a point which will feature in a later chapter when we discuss modern practice.

In penciled notes on the back pages of his personal copy of his book, *The English Bowman,* he comments of the loose,

> drawing gently but firmly, without suffering the hand to give [move] forward or feet or head to move. Keep the fingers rather open so as not to draw the string round. Shoot in compass if the Mark is not point-blank or very high. Shoot thus to the Mark.

Thomas Roberts was a very competent archer who, as did Ascham before him, regularly noted the effect of wind upon his shooting, together with much other contemporary detail. His notes which appear have been transcribed and published within a recent *Journal of the Society of Archer-Antiquaries.*[13]

Roberts comments on the practice by some, particularly it would seem in Lancashire, for fletching three arrows with right wing feathers and three with left wing to be used appropriately in cross wind conditions. A "pair" of arrows in that county was normally three (two plus a spare); therefore, this arrangement of six arrows was called a "double pair."

Roberts gives advice on those arrow weights considered right for various distances. Thus, for roving and flight shooting with a self-yew bow at twelve score (240 yards), arrows of 3s.6d weight (roughly 325 grains at the time) were right; for every score (20 yards) less in distance, he recommends that 6d. in weight be added. With a backed bow of ruby wood or fustic, however, from fourteen score (280 yards) to nine score (180 yards), weights of 3s 6d to 4s 6d were appropriate; from nine score to seven score, 6s to 6s 6d; and from six score (120 yards), 7s to 7s 6d (roughly 696 grains at that time), suggesting variations in the quality of backed bows. Arrows at that time were weighed against silver coinage in order to produce a set that matched.

Thomas Roberts is concerned, as was Ascham, with elementary aiming through the lifted bow arm and he offers several variations drawn from the practices of contemporary (eighteenth-century) archers. Some he says, make use of the knuckles of their bow hand as a gradation of scale, when the target or mark was at no great distance, looking at the first or second knuckle or even the third. The bow needed to be canted for this and it is earlier noted that the best shots are made with an upright bow. Other archers who wore gloves on their bow hands marked them with colored lines. This arrangement is interesting, since it marks the first recorded occasion when sighting, although rudimentary, was employed as an aid to aiming. Marking of bow limbs had yet to come.

Roberts is evidently interested in determining distance for accurate shooting, and with this in mind he draws attention to a book[14] published a few years earlier by Richard Oswald Mason, a patriotic citizen, in which he advocated the return of the longbow, associated with the pike—an updated version of William Neade's "double-armed man." In order to judge distance accurately, Mason suggests extending the bow arm fully, holding a braced bow, to compare the height of objects from top to bottom at different known distances to the upper limb of the bow, when seen over the bow hand, and memorizing these. He observes that by fixing the various memories in the mind an "archer may check distances with considerable precision." While recording this novel idea, Roberts declines to comment; perhaps he was unconvinced, since Mason was not an archer when he put forward the idea.

Roberts writes of "point blank" archery, and it is interesting to notice that in the late eighteenth century he reports this to be 30 yards; seemingly short by the standard of present-day traditional archery, when 50 yards would not be unusual. However, butt shooting was practiced in the late eighteenth century, and the next butt distance after 30 yards was 60 yards. Roberts may therefore be distinguishing a shot at 30 yards from one at 60 yards. Alternatively the shorter distance resulted perhaps from the practice then of drawing to the ear and not below the chin, resulting in a shallower angle between eye, nock, and arrow pile than today, and a consequent lower trajectory. The comment remains enigmatic, particularly since bow draw-weights were if anything stronger, giving greater cast than bows in the nineteenth century.

In passing, Roberts includes a note concerning a curious sighting arrangement made by an early member of the Woodmen of Arden. Mr Dilke, he reports,

> In shooting the nine score takes his aim by means of a string about 3 inches long suspended from the sleeve of his bow arm, at which there is a knot which he brings in line with the centre of the clout, and his arrow generally falls within a bows length of the centre.

The importance of the accurate pairing of arrows by weight had long been recognized, and tables were published purporting to advise on weights appropriate to distance. From Thomas Roberts we learn of late eighteenth- and early nineteenth-century belief.

A few years later Thomas Waring approached aiming "geometrically."[15] He realized, as did all archers, that an arrow aimed directly at the mark will often fly either to the left or, less frequently, to the right. Although the reason is not explained in his *Treatise* and may not have been fully understood, the circumstance is illustrated. Waring explains it by imagining a triangle consisting of a line drawn between the mark and the eye, from the eye to the ear, and from the ear to the mark. Then, he says, imagine another line, from the arrow point to the eye, from the eye to the ear, and from the ear to the point. It would follow that if the left line of the smaller triangle were to be placed on the line of the longer triangle, then the point would appear to the right of the mark.

This explanation, although ingenious, takes no account of the relative stiffness (spine) of the arrow and its ability to bend around the bow upon release. A feature which, together with gradation of spine, we recognize today as the reason for the "archer's paradox."

Waring says little more about the act of aiming, other than warning against looking at the mark along the arrow shaft.

Matters had moved on a little by 1854 when Thomas Aldred published his little book *The Young Archer's Assistant*. This featured some very rudimentary advice on aiming; the aspirant young archer is advised that "aim" is just what a boy does when he throws a stone at a bird, a coachman does with a four-horse whip, or a fisherman with a fly-rod. In each case he says, the hand obeys the eye.

To aim with the arrow point he says is "entirely out of the question" since because of the width of the bow, the arrow leaves the string at a different angle to that when drawn up—an appreciation of the circumstance, but still without a full understanding of the part played by arrow whippiness, or spine.

It is to Horace Ford that we must now turn for logical discussion on aiming, and to a rather lesser extent on sighting as an aid to aiming. It would be true to say that his contribution to the practical understanding of the act of shooting ranks with that of Ascham four hundred years earlier. For it was Ford who recognized the problem caused by drawing to the ear, then the long established form of draw. Changing the position of the drawing hand from ear to under the aiming eye, although radical and introduced against some opposition will, as he expounded, and as we shall see, improve the prospect of scoring.

Ford takes as his example a man shooting a rifle. He draws attention to the positioning of the gun and to the eye, looking directly at the mark along the barrel of the weapon. If this produces a successful result for the shooter, he argues, then why should it not for an archer? He therefore advocates moving the drawing hand, and thus the arrow nock, from the ear to beneath the eye.

He is dismissive of those who use sighting aids, those who "make a pin cushion of their left hand by inserting pins into a piece of leather, each one acting as an aiming aid." Sights as aids to aiming have no place in Ford's philosophy. He does approve however of those who put a piece of stick in the ground and use it as a "point of aim."[16] One is reminded of Ascham's comment upon this simple practice. Ford concludes by asserting as an "incontrovertible axiom" in archery that true shooting can never be accomplished excepting when the whole length of the arrow lies directly beneath the axis of the aiming eye, and by implication this suggests acceptance of left handed archery, a phenomenon actively discouraged in earlier times.

He devotes a thirteen-page chapter of his book to the subject of "eye above arrow" and although, as we shall see, not all established archers were convinced by his argument, he nevertheless hoped that having read it, the untainted young would take his advice.

The Reverend Merewether, writing four years later in *The Archer's Guide* in 1860 is also concerned with aiming and not at all with sighting, even if he understood its principle. He is of the old school however and, dismissing Ford and his theory, is concerned exclusively with drawing the arrow to the ear and not to the eye, "as many suppose;" the archer looking a little to the left of the knuckles. The pile, he says, should not be aligned with the eye or the mark for to do so would result in the arrow flying left.

With the principle of "eye above arrow" generally accepted as the older generation gave way to the next, there was a slowly growing interest in sighting devices designed to aid aiming. Firstly—as decried by Ford—by attaching pins to gloves, but later by affixing a pin to the bow limb itself. This simple forerunner of the modern bow-sight was innovated in the late 1870s by James Spedding, a knowledgeable and forward-thinking member of the Royal Toxophilite Society.[17]

Although Spedding's arrangement was noticed by his fellow archers, none is recorded as having adopted a similar device. His bow-sight consisted of a bright colored bead fixed to the bow in such a way that it could be moved as needed either horizontally or vertically; the object being to adjust it to cover the target center at each target distance. He evidently found it helpful in improving his scores; although he often remarked when he used it at public meetings that he wished the judge would ban it as "he would then know there was something in it."

As we shall later see, although Spedding was among the earliest of those to use a bow-mounted pin sight, he was soon joined by American inventors and with them inevitably we enter the age of add-on aids—those expensive accessories without which no modern archer feels properly equipped.

Before we move further into aiming aids however, we should notice that there were those who disdained progress, preferring to stay firmly rooted in the past. One such was the "expert" writing in Peck and Snyder's New York 1878 catalogue who has his own forthright advice to offer in the matter of draw, aim, and release. "Never suffer yourself to shoot with the right hand below the top of the right ear." It is easier he says for a novice to shoot with right hand low, but he will never be a good and graceful archer doing thus. Do not attempt to take sight, he warns, but when the mind thinks that the arrow is properly directed then let fly.

He mentions in passing that the point blank range of a fifty-pound bow is "not over twenty-six yards." Before dismissing that remark as absurd we should remember that he wrote for those who drew to the ear. Drawing to the chin and beneath the eye as Ford had advised would have doubled that distance and more.

In considering this, and other "expert" advice we should not, from our superior knowledge decry what they said; they wrote of that which they had been taught, long before the science of archery had been established.

Fortunately for those who declined Peck and Snyder's expert's advice, alternative help was at hand from those acknowledged practical American archers Maurice and Will Thompson. Their *How to Train in Archery*, published a year later was a fifty-page book of instruction concerned largely with advice on shooting the "York," or long distance target round. Although offering useful and relevant advice, interestingly they differentiate drawing of the arrow for short and long distance shooting. "For short distances the archer naturally draws higher with his right hand near his ear, whilst at the longer distance he lowers that hand to the level of his chin." There is no recognition of the location of the arrow beneath the eye.

The chapter titled "Keeping a Line" takes no account of arrow whippiness (spine), or the matching of arrow to bow, requiring merely that shooting is conducted "in the vertical plane of the Gold."

While much of the Thompsons' advice follows that of earlier writers, that for the loose is reflective of modern Western practice and the associated "follow through." "Merely to straighten the fingers and let the string go free," they correctly say, will "give a clumsy and sluggish loose, but the fingers should be brought smoothly backward and be pulled off the string by the force of the draw."

We turn now to Colonel Walrond, a man of military manner and bearing whose views were respected both as a successful archer and a discerning coach. His *Archery for Beginners*, from which we have already noted extracts, is based upon a lifetime of experience, and the concluding chapter of his book, "Final Advice" succinctly summarizes points he has made. Reiterating "drawing" he stresses

> remember to use both arms at the same time. Grip the bow when fully drawn. Use plenty of forefinger. Bring the right hand directly to the chin and not to the right or left of it, holding both head and drawing elbow up. Stand tall and upright and do not overdraw.

In loosing, grasp the bow tightly and keep the left hand up. Keep the right hand tight to the chin and do not drop it. Keep the right elbow up and back. After the loose keep both hands in position until the arrow has hit the target (or the ground).

Photograph of an archer used in *Archery for Beginners* to demonstrate "good style." The archer is thought to be H. H. Palarait. *(Author)*

Walrond says nothing about sighting aids, advising only that the pile of the arrow should be located and kept on the centre of the point of aim, wherever or whatever that might be. He belonged to the school which saw the point of aim—with its attendant need to concentrate on holding the bow at full draw—as a more assured way of keeping a length than reliance upon a sight, whatever form it might take. He was not disposed to part company with Ascham. Many modern traditionalists will agree.

Stanley Spencer and his "system"[18] will be the next and last expert we will consult. We have already seen his advice on standing, holding the bow and drawing, and he too is forthright in his views. He has no regard for sighting as an aid to aiming and is concerned exclusively with the point of aim—which we will designate, as he does, the p.o.a. When aiming he advises that both eyes be kept open for then, he believes, vision is clearer.

There are two reasons that cause archers to believe they should shut other than the aiming eye; one reason is that, holding the bow so erect that the string and bow when drawn interfere with the line of vision. The other is that when eyes are focused on the arrow pile whilst checking the p.o.a. [point of aim] the closeness of the pile blurs vision of both p.o.a. and target.

Archers will judge the comment for themselves.

He offers no solution for this problem—if indeed it is a problem—merely remarking that, "after correcting these faults their troubles will be ended." He goes on to stipulate that the point of aim (p.o.a.) should always be in line with the target and right eye (assuming the bow held in the left hand); a sinistral archer had yet to be accepted.

Spencer advises arrows that are perfectly matched to the bow for spine and in this he is leading the field, since the science and the purpose of spining was then in its infancy. He does not develop the reason however, always supposing that he fully understood; the opportunity to discuss the archer's paradox is therefore missed.

He remarks that, "when drawing and aiming, look directly at the p.o.a.—which should always be in line with the target—raise the bow until the arrow comes to the line between eye and the p.o.a., then hold long enough to align the arrow to the target and the p.o.a.; when fully satisfied that all is well, without conscious effort, release. Keep the mind fixed upon the release to the exclusion of all else, but do not cease aiming upon release, continue holding and aiming. Do not drop the bow-arm before the arrow reaches its destination." In this he is in agreement with Col Walrond—as are many of today's coaches.

Spencer writes colloquially and is not always easily understood. However, the core ethic of his system is relaxation; and with this message he has advanced a fundamental principle of good shooting.

With Spencer we are reaching the last of those who wrote specifically for the longbow. Within a year or two the steel bow would have made its appearance, and colored the advice given aspirant archers. It is time to stop.

Before leaving the subject entirely however we should look at that transient of phenomena, the detachable longbow sight.

The practice of marking the bow limb in some form to indicate elevation was widespread in the nineteenth and twentieth
centuries; either rings drawn around the bow limb, or a series of
differently colored dots. Three marks were usual, corresponding
to the distances of the American round of 60, 50, and 40 yards,
or two for the British Ladies National Round of 60 and 50
yards. It was the simplest form of sighting aid to aiming, and was
effective although it suffered from not being adjustable. No
allowance could be made for varying conditions of weather or
location.

To improve matters the concept of an adjustable sight was
introduced and, although disregarded by British archers, was
developed by Abner Shephardson, a respected American bow
maker. Although regarded initially as a gimmick it gained favor
and respectability in 1925 when, while using an example, Dr.
Paul Crouch became national champion.

A simple device, it consisted of a brass ring clamped securely
to the bow limb above the handle. Brazed to the ring was a slen-
der brass rod five inches in length with a horizontal "slider" projecting to the left and incorporating a "peep hole." The upright
rod was bent slightly to compensate for the angle at which the
bow is habitually held. Although effective, its use was confined to
comparatively short distances.

A more sophisticated device was then created by Arthur
Lambert, archer and author of *Modern Archery* (1932).[19] This consisted of a brass ring clamped to the bow limb above the handle
having a narrow, thin flat bar some six inches long, with a central channel extending along its length. A threaded bolt held this
to the ring. Along the edge of the central channel were graded
marks. At the base of the vertical bar a pointer, bent at the end,
was affixed. The advantage of this adaptation lay in the facility of
the pointer to be moved up or down, and from one side to the
other, enabling its use for longer distances.

An interesting variant of sighting aid was a form of backsight
incorporated into the bow string, a feature with modern conno-
tations. This was a simple knot, used in the fashion of the backsight of a rifle or a crossbow. This device could and did improve

scores when used by competent archers, and was allowed by authority, although the majority of those competing chose either simple bow marks or points of aim.

A "range," or p.o.a. recorder, was, and may still be, used by some who shoot the simple weapon. Lambert offers an example.[20] He suggests a thin piece of wood some five inches long. To record the position of an existing p.o.a., he advises, stand at the shooting line and, shutting the left eye, bring the wood to the vertical position so that the head of an extended arrow is sighted a fraction beneath the gold of the target. Holding this position, carefully run the eye down the side of the wood until reaching the p.o.a. Mark this position, making sure that the distance is recorded. To use on unfamiliar ground, raise the "finder," locate the gold with the top of the finder and, noting the position of the mark on the ground, have your p.o.a. installed.

It may not be generally known that up to and including 1954, Fédération Internationale de Tir à l'Arc (F.I.T.A., now World Archery Federation), the accepted authority for international archery, prohibited pin sights at world championship tournaments. In that year Article XVI agreed to at the subsequent business meeting, summarized: "Simple bow sights other than diophric (lens) allowed. String attachments not exceeding 1 cm allowed. P.o.a. allowed as now. Draw check indicators now allowed." Until then, points of aim alone were permitted.[21]

In passing, the British Long Bow Society, arbiters of traditional target and clout shooting, permit either marks on the limb or a movable elastic band protruding not more than 1/8 inch beyond the limb, with arrows invariably to be shot off the hand.

And so, with these proscriptions duly noted, we move next to look in detail at some of the equipment used.

FIVE

Necessary Tackle

"If you come into a shoppe and find a bowe that is small, longe, heavy and stronge, lyinge streighte, not windinge, not marred with knotte, gaule, winde shake, wen, freat or pinch, bye that bowe of my war- rante."—Roger Ascham, *Toxophilus*

In the last four chapters we have looked at the five essential aspects of the shot—the stance, nock, draw, hold and loose— as defined by sixteenth-century archer Roger Ascham, and to these we have added aiming and sighting. In this chapter we will look at the equipment used and how it has changed across the centuries—the bows and arrows, arm-guards, pouches, and quiv- ers. There are not many radical alterations possible to the simple stick and string; but nonetheless, changes were introduced, as we shall see.

Where information is known, we will also introduce the bow and arrow makers themselves.

We who live in England know little of the way in which our Saxon forbears shot, and even less about the equipment available to them; what remnants so far found suggest that bows—the old English *bogan*—were simple, short, of longbow style and of com- paratively light poundage. Although doubtless used primarily for hunting, we can infer from manuscript sources their regular use in warfare.[1]

The horn bow (*hornboga*) referred to in Saxon literature is thought to have been that carried by mounted nomad warriors and also used by Anglo-Saxon nobility for hunting. There seems no evidence of its employment in battle. However, speculatively, the bow used at the battle of Maldon by a well-connected hostage may perhaps have been superior to the simple stick and string of the *fyrd* bowman by his side.[2]

In passing, while there are just two Anglo-Saxon words for the bow, neither of which defines its purpose, there are a number for the arrow, several of which do: *strael, flan, scytel, pil, hilde-naedre* (war snake—a kenning), *herestrael, waelpil, waepenstrael* (war arrow), and *heorufla* (deadly arrow). Each of these concerns its use in warfare and confirms that, although subsidiary to the main event, where hand-to-hand combat was employed, the bow and its arrow were important in battle. In passing, an alternative expression for an Anglo-Saxon bowman (*bogaman*) was *straelbora*, literally arrow bearer or arrow man—a term used in medieval times to describe those who kept the king's peace in the ancient Gloucestershire forest of Kingswood.

While no known examples of Saxon bows or arrows survive, those of Norse origin recovered from sites at Nydam in Schleswig, Denmark, and elsewhere may well share similarity of style; and a brief description of these recorded by an English archer over a century ago may help in the understanding of those in later Saxon use.[3]

The bows he saw were from 5 feet, 7 inches (170cms) to 8 feet (187cms) in length—a wide range—with diameters from 2.8 cm to 3 cm, tapering from the centre to each end. Bellies he reported were flat and backs rounded. This of course is the opposite shape from the conventional one we are used to. Wood used was largely fir, with some yew, and was cut from saplings rather than the bole of a mature tree.

Our reporter noticed no string grooves on the limbs; strings appeared to be held in place by permanent knotting in shallow shoulders or—in at least one case—by a brass button. He estimated draw weights of those he saw at around 50 pounds, but he was not allowed to hold them.

The arrow shafts were of straight-grained coniferous wood, with evidence—he thought—of having been cleft rather than sawn. Lengths varied between 29 inches (7.3cms) and 37 inches (90cms)—again a wide variation. They were barreled in profile and the string nocks were large and "knobbed" to allow drawing fingers to grasp them in order to hold the arrow to the string. They were four-fletched with feathers four to five inches (10 cm to 13cm) long. Each was held within a narrow groove cut into the shaftment and bound with thin thread wound spirally around them.

Mrs. Butt, a nineteenth-century champion lady archer. The accoutrements hanging from her belt include a quiver, scorebook, pencil, and tassel for arrrow cleaning. (*Author*)

It was also noticed that a number of the arrow shafts appeared to bear markings, and he records a number of these. Some appear to be runic, among them those featuring what may be the runes for *gebo* (a gift), *algiz* (protection), and *teiwaz* (victory). Each arrow—it would seem—was thus personalized in a way relevant to its purpose.

Some arrowheads were of bone, but the majority were ferrous—mostly tanged although a few of those he examined were socketed. Weights of arrows differed according to the shape of head; the heavier were leaf shaped, while others were lighter, slim and pointed like awls for penetration of mail.

Moving forward through the mist of time, and taking the Norman Conquest in our stride, we meet the bow and arrow as they slowly achieve maturity in warfare. An early example of the effective use of archers in a post-conquest battle took place near Northallerton in 1138[4] when the forces of Northumberland defeated those of the Scottish King David, using archers as the first line of defense against the advancing Scottish troops. Here we have a foretaste of what was to come, when in later years the great war-bow came to dominate the military scene and English and Welsh bowmen reigned supreme on foreign battlefields.

But we must first look at other things. In an earlier chapter we were introduced to the enigmatic "turkie" bow and noted that its close association with hunting suggested its purpose. The few references there are span the centuries, for they range between a reference by Geoffrey Chaucer in his romantic poem *Romance of the Rose*, where we learn it is straight and (at least in his poem) decorated, and the inventories of sixteenth-century King Henry VIII where in Westminster a large number of "Turquy bowes of *stele* (sic)"[5] are held in the custody of one Hans Hunter, armorer to the king. Two enigmas in one, for are these possibly early steel bows?

Two other references occur in various inventories. At Westminster, kept in the "Closet next to the king's Privy Chamber" were "eight boltes for a turquybowe" (bolt and arrow were synonymous terms at the time). While in the "Litle Studie called the Newe Library" was a "Turquey Bowe with a quyver and arrowes in it."

As a preferred and perhaps specialized hunting bow the turkie/turquye bow shares its place with the bough bow and the birding bow, each used by forest dwellers in earlier days. The term does not appear in dictionaries of medieval or Tudor words and it seems therefore to have been a colloquial expression, much as the term longbow once was.

Remaining with inventories of archery material, the fifteenth century offers rich pickings, for in or about 1435 (the date is unclear) lists were made of archery material belonging to Sir John Dynham of the Arundell family,[6] minor Cornish nobility and owners of Wardour Castle. These inventories are detailed and particularly explicit of the large stocks of arrows that he possessed. They are of great interest for the detail they provide of contemporary fletchings, of arrow decoration, and of the names given their heads.

Also included are bows; and once more we find a baffling description, for eight are listed as "wood bows." If this is to distinguish them, then it is not clear from what other type of bow they are being distinguished; unless perhaps from cross bows. Six "round" bows are also included and once again we have a mystery. Here there may be a tenuous solution, however, since the term "round bow" was used by our anonymous Frenchman when he advised this type for distance shooting.

We are on safer ground when considering the arrows. Feathers for fletchings were taken from the grey goose, the white goose, and the swan; but by far the greater number was from peacocks and peahens. Those fletched with the grey goose feather were cross-nocked, yet another enigma which we shall endeavor to explain later.

Where mentioned, nocks were of "whole horn," and in one case "long horn." Some were described as "powdered." The term can mean decorated but in this case may have meant deteriorated.

Those arrows that did not have full horns were cross-nocked as mentioned above; and it is possible that by this is meant a transverse cut across the nock groove to take a horn insert.

A small number of shaftments were richly decorated, with gold interleaving the feathers, and with bindings of gold thread. Feathers varied in length, those of nine inches seem excessive but are perhaps indicative of prestige.

Many of the arrows were headed and here again there are puzzles since they do not match our own terms or descriptions. Mentioned are "culvertail," "duck bill," including "long duck bill," "pearhead bolt," "broadhook," "broadhead," "hooked," "spearhead," and "byker." It is possible to deduce some shapes and perhaps even purpose, from these brief identities. If pearhead describes a shape, then it may be that which we know today as a horn blunt. Spearhead is not too difficult to envisage and, with imagination also duckbill. Culver is an archaic word for dove and culvertail would supposedly mean "dovetail." We are familiar enough with these.

The byker head is particularly interesting however. If byker is cognate with "bicker" then in earlier times this word was defined as "an assault with arrows." A byker head might therefore be a lighter head designed for mass delivery. However it might also mean "beak" and be a penetrating point.

The purpose of this extensive collection is unclear; but the quality of the fletches, the use of peahen, peacock, and swan feathers, and the gold decoration suggests quality material for sport; and sport in the fifteenth century meant just one thing—hunting and the chase. Illustrations within the hunting books are explicit about the use of the longbow and the crossbow, and arrows—where depicted—are invariably barbed broadheads.

Leaving the fifteenth century for the sixteenth, and a Tudor dynasty that favored the bow, we are fortunate on two important counts. Firstly by having expert opinion and advice on both shooting and the equipment necessary for this purpose, provided by Roger Ascham in 1545; and secondly, through the intervention of fate, much of the equipment itself following the sad loss of the Royal flagship, *Mary Rose*, off Spithead, Portsmouth, in that same year.

Within previous chapters we have carefully considered Ascham's advisory comments and compared them with the views of others, of lesser standing who, over the years, have claimed expertise. It is time now to look in detail at the bows and arrows with which Ascham was so familiar. And we will begin with the bow.

The Anthony Roll, within which the equipment carried by Henry VIII's warships was listed, shows there to have been a total of two hundred and fifty "bowes of yeugh" on board the *Mary Rose*. Of this number a total of 180 have been recovered—eight in the nineteenth century and 172 in modern times. Of those 172, 138 are complete, and of these some 120 have been closely examined. Details of this analysis are contained within the *Mary Rose* archaeological report "Weapons of Warre" Part 2.[7]

All exceed six feet in length, with those of six feet, five inches in the majority. All are made with variants of the D section, variously described as "slab sided," "round D section," "flat D section," and "trapezoidal." A mysterious feature of many are peck marks on the left of the upper limb, adjacent to, but not corresponding with, either the geometric center or the center of gravity. These bowyer's marks may identify individuals or perhaps their guilds, although there are no known written references to confirm this.

It is unclear whether these were solely to denote upper limbs or whether they had an as yet undiscovered function. It is interesting that in just one case markings in the shape of a chevron are on the right side of the limb—an aberration perhaps, but it is tempting to speculate its use for a left handed archer. The layout of these marks varies, but in eleven cases six dots are parallel—three and three—with the seventh above and central to them. The effect of this is to produce a steeple shape, a shape that may perhaps be the origin of the steeple shaped arrow-pass formed of mother-of-pearl familiarly found on modern longbows of self-yew.

The upper and lower tips of many of the bows are marked with single grooves, cut into the wood on opposite sides, top and bottom. At first these were believed to have been notches cut to held the string while "tillering" the bow in the course of its construction (i.e., when checking for even bending of the limbs). Current belief, based upon observation, is that these grooves result from the cutting of a side groove, technically a side nock or notch, into the horn tip to accommodate the bow string, the cut passing through the horn and slightly into the wood. The clue to this belief arose from examination of a side-nocked eighteenth century bow in the possession of the author. This feature is believed to aid stringing in a heavy draw-weight weapon. It no longer exists in modern bow making.

Draw weights of these sixteenth century weapons can only be estimated, since they have been immersed in seawater for over five centuries. However many representations have been made using the technical data available from analysis of the originals, and variations of between 90 and 160 pounds have been achieved. This accords broadly with the theoretical approximations of actual bows, which range between 98 and 150 pounds, and are derived from calculations of girth, length, and mass.

All bows recovered from the ship have been of yew, reflecting Roger Acham's contemporary comment, "As for brazil wood, elm, wych and ash, experience doth prove them to be but mean for bows, and so to conclude, yew of all things is that whereof perfect shooting would have bows made."

To simplify, the sap wood of yew provides tension and its heart wood compression, making it a natural spring. It is favored for its excellent modulus of elasticity, its better ability to bend and return than other woods.

While bows were undoubtedly also made from English timber, unless it was grown in large plantations with trees close together and carefully tended to remove shoots and pins it would have grown knotty and twisted and of little or no value for weapons. Yew of suitable quality was imported from Spain and northern Italy in considerable quantity and from the Baltic and Adriatic countries as well, while a sizeable trade between Ireland and the port and city of Bristol provided yew for that city's bowyers.[8]

Makers of longbows were, and are, craftspeople of the highest order, and today many of the finest are members of the Craft Guild of Traditional Bowyers and Fletchers, an organization formed nearly thirty years ago. Closely linked with the original two London Livery Companies associated with these skills, members of the Guild maintain their ancient traditions of quality.[9]

Although the inventory of the Dynham arrows provides much welcome information, and we know of their fletchings, nocks and heads, none remain for us to view; we have no shafts to tell us of profiles. Matters are different when we come to the sixteenth century, for from the *Mary Rose* many hundreds have been recovered; and after careful reclamation, profiles, lengths, and material are there to be examined at will.

Five profiles are recognizable, four being familiar enough to traditionalists of today: the straight, the bob-tailed, the breasted, and the barreled; but one is not, the saddled, or doubly barreled profile, no longer in use today. Examination of examples seems to show a possible flight advantage combined with additional front-end strength, however it would have been far more difficult to make than other profiles and it has not survived.

Mary Rose arrows were of a number of woods, each genus possessing its own properties of elasticity and weight. Sixteenth century military archers would have had to call upon innate skills when coping with the peculiarities of each. From 2,303 complete shafts, 646 were deemed suited to detailed examination as samples; of these 501 were of poplar, ninety of birch, thirty-eight of alder, seven of willow, thirty-two of hornbeam, two of either birch or poplar, and one each of hawthorn and ash. The spread is particularly interesting in the light of Roger Ascham's stated preference for ash as a military shaft above all other woods.

Lengths vary between 28 inches and 30 inches with a few shorter and others longer. No arrowheads have survived, although the oxidized image of one suggests a London Museum Type 16 (Jessop M4)[10], a lightly and closely barbed broad-head. If this were the preferred head then it suggests that targets for seaborne archers may have been the sailor crews of enemy vessels rather than the soldiers that might be carried. Seamen would be susceptible to an arrowhead which remained in their bodies. No fletchings remain, but evidence from the marks left by bindings suggests lengths broadly between 6 inches and 8 inches.

If the archaeological report is to be believed, string grooves (nocks) varied in depth between 2mm and 6.19mm, with widths varying between 1.8mm and 5.3mm, dimensions difficult to associate with the circumferences of (later) hempen bow strings, and suggesting that many arrows were held on strings by gripping between fore and second finger. Horn protective inserts were fitted to many shafts and a (very) few have survived. These are similar to today's nock pieces.

Personal to archers is their arm-guard or bracer—the term derives from the Latin *bracchia*: arm. Although it is evident that not all *Mary Rose* bowmen wore one, nevertheless we will devote a line or two to their function and, since we have a number

Reproductions of bracers found aboard the *Mary Rose*. Note the variety of decoration: sunburst (left); rose (right); royal arms with surrounding Ave (center). (*Author*)

recovered from the warship we will look at one or two examples.[11]

Twenty-four bracers were recovered from the warship and of these twenty-one are more or less whole; the remaining three are fragmentary and include one of horn. With the exception of one of ivory, the complete ones are all of leather, mostly bovine.

A bracer or arm-guard probably remained with an archer during his whole shooting life, and any decoration present might reveal something of his personality, or his affiliation. Thus, religious symbolism in the form of a crucifixion appears on one and Marion *aves* on two others. Association with a guild is suggested by at least one, where a grid-iron symbol of the Girdlers Company is stamped. St Peter's keys—symbol of Exeter Cathedral—may indicate the origin of the owner, while at least two, and possibly others have royal insignia. The rose appears on several, suggestive of the Tudor emblem, or even personalized association with the ship.

Of particular interest is an ivory example, a fine and unique piece which was found attached to a right forearm. The bracer was however small, as was its wearer. If the owner were indeed an archer then this would indicate left-handedness—not a welcome characteristic at any time, and especially so on board ship. The circumstance is a little perplexing.

And so, with an unsolved Tudor puzzle behind us we will slip forward into the seventeenth century and, sadly, to a dearth of equipment for study.

The glut of sixteenth-century archery material available for study leaves us ill-prepared for the paucity that is to follow. For although recreational archery thrived, at least for a time, through the support and personal interest of King Charles II and the activity of the Society of Finsbury Archers—just one item of consequence remains to intrigue. This, the Renishaw Hall bow, whose early history is largely undocumented and which was known for many years as "Robin Hood's Bow," we will now consider; and we will draw upon a monograph prepared for the Society of Archer Antiquaries in 2011 by member Michael Leach.[12]

The bow is laminated and consists of a yew belly, a back believed to be hickory and a core laminate that may be of wych elm. The tips are damaged and there are no stringing horns, although there is evidence for cone shaped ends that, undamaged, could have accommodated them. The length now is 68 inches, suggesting an original length of 70 inches. There is evidence for scarfing of the core laminate, a feature of some later, eighteenth century bows; however the weapon is known to have been damaged when dropped in 1949 and this may reflect repair work then.

Of particular interest is the presence of a number of small indents forming a "steeple" pattern on the upper limb by the arrow pass. These show similarity with bowyers marks previously noted on sixteenth century bows where they seem to indicate the upper limb and also perhaps identify the maker; their presence on the Renishaw bow may thus be the mark of a Yorkshire bow maker. In addition, the back of each limb has a protruding knot, cleverly incorporated within the profile of the bow, and on each of these there are short diagonal knife cuts, the purposes of which are unknown. The bow has an estimated draw weight of 60 pounds.

The original owner is unknown, but there are associations with the families of Rodes and Armytage; and it is of passing interest that the name Rodes appears on the Roll of the Honourable Artillery Company of London[13] whose association with seventeenth-century archery was considerable. However, there we will leave speculation.

Although there is a dearth of seventeenth century artifacts we are a little luckier with the eighteenth century; for a small number of bows survive. Five are within the writer's collection and can be examined in detail. First, and earliest, is an unusual "hinged" or "carriage" bow thought to have been converted from a self yew weapon. Now 72 1/2 inches overall in length, it is of conventional tapered, straight sided section with convex belly. It has a wrought iron and ornamented brass hinge, identified as of early eighteenth century form. When acquired it was missing both stringing horns; these were replaced by nineteenth century examples. Its provenance is unknown and its purpose can only be surmised as a gentleman's hunting weapon. It is tentatively dated by its decoration to the early years of the eighteenth century and is a rare example of the genre. It is even possible that in its original condition it was a survivor of the seventeenth century.

For the next we turn to Scotland and a recreational bow by Thomas Grant of Edinburgh. Grant, who lived well into his nineties, was a prolific maker of archery equipment and, although not a recognized bow maker to the Royal Company, its members sought and used his bows. He was a bowyer of the "old school" and his weapons incorporated two interesting archaic features—the side nock and the belly wedge.

The bow is of conventional longbow style, made of self lancewood, 71 inches in length with a flat back and a convex belly; it has no riser and would have come around in full compass. The handle covering includes decorative silver wire.

The belly wedge was designed to avoid damaging the arrow if it were pulled beyond its proper draw length. Rather than its point becoming jammed into the back of the bow it would slide over the triangle of the wedge and do no harm. The side cut string grooves in the nock are a reflection of those on sixteenth-

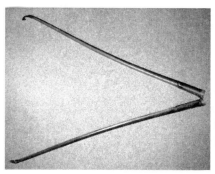

Left, an unusual "carriage" bow hinged at the center. Right, a belly wedge. (*Author*)

century bows; they incorporate "purging holes" cut into the horn to avoid the effect of hydraulic pressure when the horns are glued into position.

This bow was originally at Blair Atholl Castle in Scotland, where for nearly two centuries it hung with others on a wall within the castle. It has provenance to an Earl of Atholl who was elected to the Royal Company of Archers (Sovereign's Bodyguard for Scotland) in December 1778.[14]

Also associated with the Royal Company are two eighteenth century arrows, these are straight self shafts, 27 inches in length, with low cut triangular fletches 4 inches long. Unusually for the period, piles are parallel and of brass. They are believed to have been made in Edinburgh where there were a number of lorimers—workers in brass—who are known to have produced arrowheads. Each is marked both "HF" and "SF" believed to denote Hugh Fraser and Simon Fraser respectively. Each was a member of the Royal Company, Hugh elected in 1749 and Simon in 1770.[15]

The third bow to be examined is by Thomas Waring the Elder who, with his employer Sir Ashton Lever, was co-founder in 1781 of the Toxophilite Society. Waring had learned the art of bow-making from a member of the Kelsal family, a long estab-lished firm of Manchester bowyers and his bows probably reflected ancient practice.

This bow is 71 inches long, and is of ruby wood backed by hickory. It has a marked draw weight of 69 pounds and is thus heavy for a recreational weapon. It has a slim handle riser but would probably have come around in full compass when drawn. Each stringing horn has a purging hole, indicating that they were bespoke to the bow; later practice was to use nocks purchased from abroad.

Waring was innovative as a bowyer, using an unconventional "T bar" method of construction. To the hickory back a central upright was fixed, extending the length of the stave; on either side of this were glued quadrants to form the belly.

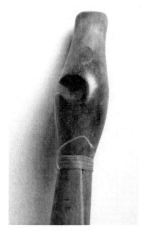

A side nock showing a filled in purging hole. The purging hole allowed excess glue to flow away from the horn to provide a stronger bond to the bow. (*Author*)

He was also closely associated with the proposal by a patriotic citizen to re-introduce the concept of combining bow and pike as a defensive weapon against a possible Napoleonic invasion; and he probably made both bow and pike, since the prototype combination was to be seen at his show room. Although the concept was potentially viable, those responsible for the security of house and home chose to rely upon musket and sword. Happily in the event neither was needed.

The fourth bow is by a provincial bowyer and is attributed to Joseph Wrigley of Cheetham, Manchester. It dates from the late eighteenth century and shows the practice of scarfing in place of the fishtail splicing of two limbs. Here, the back and the belly are each of a self piece, with the core laminate consisting of two pieces scarfed together at the handle. It is a system which did not survive much beyond the cusp of that century.

The bow, whose lower limb has been shortened, at present measures 68 1/4 inches between nocks. The lower limb nock has been replaced, while the upper nock is original and is inscribed with the number 45, and it has a purging hole. The draw weight of the bow is 45 pounds. The initials J H W are marked on the upper limb. The belly is of yew, the core laminate is fustic, and the back is of hickory. The handle covering is a light green velour.

Moving now into the early nineteenth century there is an increase in the number of aspirant bow makers and from these we will select just five, two from Scotland, and three from provincial English bowyers. Of these two will be from Bath in Somerset and one from Preston, near Manchester. The reason for including a fifth bow will be apparent later.

We will begin by looking at a bow by William Ainsworth, a bowyer of Walton le Dale, Preston, near Manchester, an excellent maker said to have been favored by Liverpool and North Welsh clubs. In common with most bow makers of the time he gave guarantees and would have exchanged a bow should it have broken within a year of "fair usage."

The construction of this bow is interesting—a combination of yew belly and hickory back with two core laminations, one of fustic or perhaps greenheart, and the other of rosewood. It has a plano-convex section and an unconventionally shaped rectangular arrow pass in mother of pearl.

It measures just 68 inches between stringing nocks of cow horn, into which purging holes, common to the period, have been bored. It has a marked draw weight of 51 pounds, and a braid handle covering which may not be original. It is in excellent condition.

Ringing the changes, we turn to Scotland for the second example of these early nineteenth-century weapons. This example is attributed to George Lindsay-Rae of Edinburgh, bower (as they were called) to the Royal Company of Archers between 1793 and 1818. Unusually we are able to date this self-yew bow with reasonable accuracy for it was commissioned by Sir Nathaniel Spens, Captain General of the Royal Company of Archers, in 1810 to mark his 60th year in archery.[16] It was awarded at a contest in that year and won by James Miller. A silver plate on the upper limb records the occasion. The weapon is of conventional plano-convex section and measures 68 inches between nocks—Scottish bows were habitually shorter than their English counterparts.

The stringing horns are of Scottish "spoon" shape and the string groove is "dished" in the manner of earlier Scottish side-nocks. The upper horn has a purging hole. There is evidence for an original belly-wedge, removed when the silver plate was attached. No draw weight is marked.

The third and fourth bows are by John Spreat the Elder[17] and his nephew, also John Spreat. Spreat senior began his archery business at Bath in the 1820s, serving gentlefolk who shot at the great houses in the neighborhood

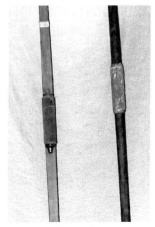

Bows by Spreat senior, right, and junior. (*Author*)

and who occasionally visited the archery grounds laid out for them within the city's Sidney Gardens. He was later joined by his nephew.

Bows made by Spreat senior are unusual, almost unique, with their elliptical section. A lady's example, 59 inches in length is described, having a draw weight of 26 pounds. It is of self lance-wood, a popular alternative to yew, and has a red velour handle. Purging holes are cut on both stringing horns. The maker advertised his daughter, Bessie, as an instructor to initiate young ladies into the art of shooting.

John Spreat the Younger is included since the writer, who knew of the family association, had made the assumption that he worked at his uncle's firm and thus would have made bows to his uncle's specification. It was known that each had their own workshop, but that was not unusual. However, the assumption was proven to be wrong, when a bow by the nephew was found and compared.

The ladies bow made by nephew Spreat is conventionally plano-convex in section. It has a handle riser with finial terminals and red velour covering. It is short, just 52 1/2 inches in length. No draw weight is marked. One horn is broken and the other is missing. It is illustrated here alongside an example of a ladies bow by Spreat the Elder.

The younger Spreat when advertising his goods mentions prominently that he is an Archer, a probable reference to a small and short-lived archery club believed to have formed in 1837 and which shot at an archery ground laid out for the purpose within the ornamental gardens at Bladud's Spa in Bath.

The fifth weapon illustrated is a man's self bow in a dark exotic tropical wood. It was made by James Reid, a bow maker of Kilwinning in Ayrshire, Scotland—home of papingo shooting (a form of popinjay) and perhaps made for that purpose. It is 64 1/2 inches in length and has an uncovered cork handle. Horn nocks of Scottish spoon shape are fitted which have purging holes.

It has an unusual section shape—twin concave grooves run the length of a flat back, over a conventional convex belly. Although uncommon, other similar bows are known but with just a single concavity extending along the back; the purpose is unknown. The writer has two others with this feature and knows of more. This bow is marked with the maker's name and the figures 28 and 25; which are taken to mean a draw length of 28 inches and a draw weight of 25 pounds.

Kilwinning was also home to David Muir, uncle to Peter Muir, champion archer and long time bower to the Royal Company. Peter was apprenticed to his uncle; and James Reid may also have begun his training in that fashion.

We will leave the early years of the nineteenth century now, and move forward to a later time. We find a period which saw the emergence of numerous bow-makers, each striving to catch a slice of the blossoming new activity of archery, now a mildly athletic indulgence acceptable to a socially hidebound leisured class; and for the later years we are overwhelmed for choice. From the many who marketed archery material I will select just six in order to illustrate those of this period; they are, for London and in no order of importance Thomas Aldred, Frederick Henry Ayres, James Buchanan and Frederick Feltham. They are joined by two popular provincial bow makers, F. W. Thompson of Meriden, and Henry Bown of Leamington.

As we have noticed earlier, Thomas Aldred, with Joseph Ainge and James Buchanan, bought the archery business of John and David Freeman in 1846. The partnership failed however and Aldred found himself alone. Although he died in 1887, while sourcing yew in the Spanish mountains, his firm continued in business until 1918 when it was absorbed into that of F. W. Ayres.

Aldred's bows were of the finest Pyrenean yew, much of it personally sourced. It was said that each weapon was five years in the making; three years seasoning the wood following the cutting of the staves, then, after glueing, a year to allow the glue to set. The staves were then roughly shaped and after a further year of tillering and preparation the bow was complete and ready to be sold. This care in manufacture is probably why so many of his bows survive today. Many of the forty bows in the author's collection are in mint condition, a testament to quality and workmanship and, judged by the quantity surviving, perhaps also among the more prolific of the nineteenth century bowyers.

The bow I have chosen to describe is of yew backed yew, and at 67 1/2 inches between nock grooves, is four inches shorter than is usual for men's bows by Aldred. It has provenance to C.J. Longman, National Champion in 1883, although another of Longman's bows in the collection measures 72 inches and is more likely to be that with which he achieved his championship. The shorter bow, which is 53 pounds in draw weight has "180 yds" marked on the lower limb, suggesting its use for clout shooting. It has a braid handle binding and—unusually for a backed bow—a mother of pearl arrow pass. Longman was co-author, with Col. Walrond and others, of *Archery* in the Badminton Library Series.[18] With the increase in demand came the need for change and this is apparent in the stringing horns. Now bought in from abroad they no longer exhibit the purging hole common to the earlier bespoke horn.

James Buchanan, briefly a partner with Aldred and Joseph Ainge, began his own business in 1847. He quickly built a reputation for excellence and was the favored bowyer of many of the better archers. It was he who was responsible for introducing the division of the bow into two separate working limbs. Hitherto bowyers had provided a simple built up handle grip—a riser—on the back of the bow. Buchanan deepened the centre belly section of his bows to provide a fully non-working handle. This feature which was quickly adopted by other bow makers, was known as the "Buchanan dips." Resulting from the innovation, bows no longer jarred in the hand, and cast was improved. Champion archer Horace Ford is said to have used only his bows.

Typical of Buchanan's work is a self-yew bow 71 inches in length and of 56 pounds draw weight. It has an arrow pass in mother of pearl, and a green velour handle, suggesting a mid-century origin. The bow is of some circumstantial interest since faintly to be seen on the back of the lower limb are the letters H A F, the initials of Horace Alfred Ford, suggesting that perhaps at some time the bow had an association with him. We shall never know. James Buchanan died in 1889 although his business continued into the twentieth century.

Next to be considered is a bow by Frederick Feltham, an erstwhile maker of gloves and minor archery requisites in the Barbican, London, who, in 1856, branched out to manufacture and supply sporting equipment. Sitting alongside bats, balls, and dumbbells now appeared bows and arrows, plus a claim, with no evidence advanced, to be the "largest maker of longbows in the kingdom." His business lasted until his death in 1910, although the archery business may have fizzled out by 1889, after which year advertising of bows and arrows had ceased.

Feltham's bows can often be distinguished by the deeper than usual handle riser, evident on the bow to be described. This is a man's self-yew weapon, well made and measuring 71 inches between nock grooves. It has a draw weight of 40 pounds marked on the limb and is of conventional plano-convex section with a green velour handle cover. No arrow pass is fitted although this is generally conventional on self-yew bows to protect the comparatively softer wood. Although priding himself on being a principal maker of yew bows, he evidently diversified, since his name appears on others, of lancewood—which he stained to resemble yew—and also laminated bows of greenheart and lemonwood.

Fourth and last of the bowyers chosen to represent the later years of London bowyery, is Frederick Henry Ayres, in business between 1889 and his death in 1904. The Ayres bow described is of self-yew, measures 71 1/2 inches between nock grooves and has a draw weight of 53 pounds. Adjacent to the draw weight mark there is inscribed in Indian ink 5 ★ 0, taken to indicate the best arrow weight for that bow. It has a braid handle and a steeple shaped arrow pass in mother-of-pearl. The section is convention-al plano-convex.

Ayres's firm was notable for the diversity of its products. Billiard tables and bagatelle boards rubbed shoulders with cro-quet and tennis tackle and archery material of every description; while latterly among its varied products were included bicycles ("velocipedes"), motor bikes, and even motor cars. Ayres senior controlled his firm personally, but after his death it continued to trade, with his eldest son, also Frederick Henry, in control. In 1948 it merged with Slazengers, Ltd.

Before we move from London to look at provincial bow-makers and their work, we should notice important develop-ments in the manufacture of arrows. Some time in the 1830s, the regular length of men's arrows changed from 27 inches (the length from before and throughout the eighteenth century revival) to 28 inches, a standard which remained until recent times. It is unknown when the earlier length was introduced, or whether this was the standard length of seventeenth century recreational shafts.

A second, and short-lived, alteration to tradition came with the introduction of the spiral fletch. Patented by Dr. McGrigor Croft, physician to Queen Victoria, this innovation was, by per-missions, named the "Alexandra Arrow" in honor of the Queen's daughter. It had a mixed reception, ladies tending to favor it for their shorter distances; but it was finally given the coup de grace by a diatribe against it from Peter Muir,[19] doyen of arrow makers.

A third noticeable change, lasting until today, was fletching shape. Until the late 1870s all arrows bore triangular fletches, an arrangement which might well have continued until today were it not for a Mr. Henry Elliott who, having broken the forward

An Alexandra style arrow. Note the spiral fletchings. (*Author*)

part of a fletching on one of his arrows chose to break the other two to match and, upon shooting them, was surprised to see the arrow flew better than others with conventionally shaped feathers. This intriguing circumstance was reported in the columns of *The Field* sporting newspaper, and was noted with interest by the principal arrow makers. It was not long before the shield shape so familiar to us today made its commercial appearance.

Returning to the bow, and representing provincial bowyery, is an example of a weapon by F. W. Thompson, of Meriden and one by Henry Bown of Royal Leamington Spa. The Woodmen of Arden who shot at Meriden, near Coventry in Warwickshire, have been served by four generations of the Thompson family of bow-makers since their origin in 1785; an almost unique tradition in modern times, equaled only by the family Purle of London.

The family had Scottish connections and a member, Dick Thompson, was maker of arrows to Peter Muir of Edinburgh. It was said that other nineteenth-century bow makers had learned their initial skills at Meriden, where the old bowyer's workshop still survives. The truth of this cannot be verified but if so, then Aldred, Bown, and Bown's colleague, Preston, may each owe their art to a Thompson.

The bow described is of self yew, 68 inches in length—short for a man's target weapon, but suited to clout shooting. Draw weight is marked at 48 pounds. It is of conventional plano-convex section, has a green braid handle covering and an arrow pass in mother-of-pearl. Although in good condition, this bow is no longer straight, since at one time it has been left strung and now "follows the string" in a permanent curve.

It is not possible to accurately date a Thompson bow since their maker's mark has remained the same through the years. However the quality of the material and the finish are consistent with work by Samuel Thompson, who died in 1882, and the bow may date to 1880 or even earlier.

Henry Bown of Leamington (1820-1886) is notable for introducing and sponsoring the Midland Counties Archery Meeting in 1851, the first such local public meeting to be established following the Grand National meeting in 1844. It was held within the Jephson Gardens, Leamington, and was an unqualified success. Bown continued to be associated with subsequent meetings until his death.

The bow described is a man's weapon of stained lancewood backed by hickory. It is 71 1/2 inches in length and of conventional section. It has a draw weight of 48 pounds and a green braid handle cover; with it came a hempen bow string, believed to be original.

This chapter has been concerned largely with bows, arrows, and their makers through the years; and we will end it by looking at two weapons in use by American archers during the latter part of the nineteenth century; one by English bowyer Philip Highfield who specialized in exporting to the United States, and the other by American bow maker E. I. Horsman.

Highfield led the field with the export of his equipment to a rapidly expanding market in America. He chose, or perhaps was chosen by, Messrs Peck and Snyder of New York, among the main suppliers of archery material to the clubs now forming or expanding during the late nineteenth century.

The firm stocked a full range of Highfield's tackle, placing particular emphasis on the quality of his bows, invoking the approval of champion archer Maurice Thompson in support.[20] In 1878 Thompson had written, "No bows in this country can equal the beautiful weapons made by Philip Highfield of London."

Matters took a different turn in 1879 however when, having been shown and then shot with a bow made by E. I. Horsman, a rival stockist also of New York, Thompson had a change of heart, commenting. "I have given your bows the hardest and most merciless test imaginable; they shoot better than any bows of the same class."[21]

The "Royal Archery" advertisement. Note good stance, but the archer appears to be pinching the arrow. (*Author*)

Since the author possesses bows by both Highfield and Horsman, it will be interesting to compare like with like, perhaps to understand the superiority of the native product.

Illustrated therefore are two bows, each in self-lancewood. That by Highfield is 70 inches long while that by Horsman is 60 1/2 inches in length. The Highfield is marked 40 pounds in draw-weight with a blue velour handle cover, the Horsman, 45 pounds with red velour handle. Each is plano-convex in section with no discernible difference in back or belly. Nock shapes are broadly similar. It might be intimated, unkindly perhaps, that Mr Horsman used Mr Highfield's bow as a model for his own.

It would be quite wrong to suggest that the American bow makers were devoid of invention, and we will conclude by briefly examining two examples of entrepreneurial initiative, which, although neither had much impact on the archery scene, show that not all bow makers were hidebound by tradition.

Firstly the "Royal Archery" bow, marketed by Perry Mason & Co. of Boston. This curious object was patented in 1879 by William Wright and G. L. Thorn, and is described as, "a take-apart bow consisting of a metal centre section comprising an annular ring having on each side hollow tapered projections into which detachable limbs are slotted."

The accompanying arrow had a two-inch metal rod inserted in the forward end and the fletches, or "wings," were either of horse hair, hair cloth, or wire hair to survive passage through the central hole. The arrow shaft was grooved to receive the wings. The bow nocks were of metal, advertised as nickeled brass.

The limbs were of second growth ash, of circular section, tapered and varnished. When marketed the bow was available in lengths of between three and six feet to which should be added—vide the advertisement—six inches to accommodate the length of the handle. This would have seemingly left the purchaser seeking an exact length in some dilemma, since three inches of each limb is within the handle.

Archery dress circa 1880. Note pouch for arrows with retaining strap and the large carrying quiver on the ground. (*Author*)

This oddity found no place on the competition circuit but was no doubt bought by the curious since a number have found their way into collections.

The second bow to be examined is also unusual. It was introduced in 1878 by Conroy, Bissett and Malleson, a firm of fishing tackle makers, and modeled upon their bamboo fishing rods. It was available in a variety of combinations of material. That in the author's collection consists of a hickory and bamboo "T bar," flanked by quadrants of lancewood; and although marked 1878 in Indian ink on the lower limb, varies from the patented description.

A woman's bow, it is 66 inches long with a draw weight of 30 pounds. Each limb is bound at regular intervals with red silk, perhaps to reflect, as it is believed, a practice used with the firm's fishing rods, to secure the eyelets for the line; here, perhaps used for decoration, or possibly to help with the integrity of the construction. The handle cover is of khaki braid. It has an unusual rectangular section and string nocks of nickeled brass.

The bow was marketed commercially and had some success with competitive archers, although complexity of manufacture restricted production in any quantity. Will Thompson said of it,

> The bow is very elastic. It has a very smooth spring when the string is loosened, giving no jar to the hand. It is absolutely unbreakable, I am satisfied of this fact. I know what I have seen, that you make a better bow than we can get from England.

This in the year that his brother was acclaiming Philip Highfield's English bows!

The nineteenth century was notable for a subtle change for that most personal of an archer's tackle, the quiver. Until late in the century, arrows for use were carried by women in a pouch and by men in a lined pocket. Spare arrows were kept in the quiver—a larger container that remained on the ground, opened only when a replacement was required. It was not until well into the twentieth century that the term "pouch" disappeared and quivers as we know them today became attached to belts. The formality of a jacket having now been discarded, men too wore a quiver.

In this chapter we have looked at many bows and their development across the centuries and the author is fully conscious that he has but scraped the surface; far more remains unrecorded. However we move on, for in the next chapter may be found details of the many and various types of scoring, the targets used and the development of standard rounds; while in the final section a modern coach with over forty years experience of the traditional recreational longbow will take the reader through the techniques of shooting the longbow.

SIX

Of Targets and Scoring

"Men doubt yet in lookeing at the marke what way is best. . . . yet it maketh no greate matter whiche way a man looke at his marke if it be joyned with (accompanied by) comelye shootinge."
—Roger Ascham, Toxophilus

I n early days, if we are to believe the ballads, archers shot towards a "garland." Quite what this was is open to question, but it was often associated with a stick of hazel or willow, a "wand;" and indeed the practice of wand shooting is still part of traditional archery today. The garland is more difficult to define—perhaps a circlet of twigs and flowers gathered from the hedgerow and mounted on an earthen butt—the wand placed within. Although there are slight clues from early writings we are left to speculate about an exact purpose.

An early appearance of the garland can be found within a ballad of Robin Hood, source of much ancient archery lore. The quote in question comes from *A Littel Geste of Robyn Hode*, a folk ballad thought to date from the early fifteenth century.

It purports to record a meeting between Robin and his king; but while we can dismiss this as fiction, we might note the activity, for it has an interesting similarity with a fifteenth-century French practice of shooting under the screen already noticed in an earlier chapter. The two stanzas concerned are:

Two yerdes [rods] there were set up,
Thereto gan they gange [went they there]
By fifty pase [paces] our kinge sayd
The markes were to longe.

Despite the king's concern, the marks stayed where they were.

On every side a rose garlande;
They shot under the lyne;
Who fayleth of the rose garlande, sayd Robyn
His takyll he shall tyne [forfeit].[1]

The forfeit for going above the line was to lose the arrow. Although our fifteenth-century Frenchman did not say as much, it seems likely that a similar forfeit was paid by those French bowmen who shot above or into the screen.

A curious and garbled sixteenth-century account of wand shooting also occurs in ballad form. This purports to describe a fictional archery challenge between Henry VIII and Queen Catherine, shot between three king's archers and Robin Hood, with two colleagues.

The fictional match takes place on Finsbury Fields at a time before archery there was regulated. The king calls for the distance to be measured accurately by line, but Robin has other ideas. "Measure no mark for us my liege," he tells the king, "we'll shoot at sun and moon." He then decides the distance: "A full fifteen score."[2] (Probably paces, perhaps 280 yards.)

Six archers compete, shooting one arrow each, turn and turn about; nearest to the mark taking the point. At the end of the first session the king's archers lead, all three having beaten Robin's team. The suggestion is however that this was pre-arranged since, knowing of the superiority of his team, he wished to win a wager. At the next session he equalizes, and then comes the denouement: his team takes the next session and the match. Although garbled, and slanted towards the exploits of our forest hero, the account offers some indication of practice at the time.

In an earlier chapter shooting hoyles is mentioned. This was a rural activity much practiced by those on their way to church or market. An adaptation of the more formal roving marks shooting, hoyles involved picking out a natural feature in the land-scape—a mole hill, a clump of grass, a bush or something readily visible some distance away at which to shoot. The nearest arrow to the target entitled the owner to pick the next mark and so on. Formal scoring was not necessarily involved, although shooting for pence was probably common. There is a reference in a ballad to this:

Robin Hood is reminded that he has neglected his church attendance and has been persuaded to visit Nottingham to renew his vows. Little John is accompanying him on their way to Nottingham and each has his bow.

> We will shoot a peney [for a penny], said Little John.
> Then shot they forth, these yemen two,
> Both at buske and brome [brush and broom]
> Till Little John won of his master
> Five shilling to hose and shoon [stockings and shoes][3]

Robin disputes this and refuses to pay up. This annoys Little John and after coming to blows they part company. A fictional example but it serves to show what was a commonplace activity.

The roving marks, popular with those who frequented Finsbury Fields for two hundred years from the late sixteenth century, were bound by formal rules, very necessary for safety. Although those individuals who shot regularly may not have formed a cohesive society, as target archers had done, neverthe-less they were deemed to have read and understood these rules. The first cohesive list was set down in 1601. Guidance was given concerning lengths between shooter and mark. "You must shoot 'long aime' because this [scores of yards] is set downe by meas-ure of the line." In other words, distance was not a matter of guesswork.

Safety was paramount with nearly two hundred marks and perhaps many groups of archers on the fields at the same time.

> You muste note, that wee have set downe the markes to be
> taken all going into the fields, and if you be coming home-ward, looke for the marke you shoot at and not for the marke

you stand at. And we have placed evey marke from left to right. And if a mark is found along a banke, alwayes look for the marke from the West towards the East.[4]

In an attempt to reduce bad temper and intemperate language whilst on the field, the rules were said to be

For the better advertisement of such as are not acquainted with the order of the game and custom of the field whereby often arise controversies and diverse times grow rash and unadvised oaths to the derogation of God's glory we have thought it good to set downe such orderes as are fittest to be observed in this exercise.[5]

There follow eight rules for guidance of this informal shooting. These rules were updated and proliferated over the years as new booklets appeared. Thus by 1628 eight had become nine; by 1676, nine had become twelve; and by 1802—the last recorded set—there were fifteen to know and remember.

Scoring was achieved by the closeness of arrows to the mark—a system similar in some ways to that for the game of bowls. Distances shot varied between nine score (180 yards), and over nineteen score (380 yards). "Seven was the game," meant that when the groups or pairs competed, as soon as a group had won seven distances, they were declared the winners.

Arising out of this form of archery is the more formal clout shooting, conducted at nine score yards (24 roods of 7 1/2 yards) for men, and seven score yards (16 roods) for women—when women took part. The Societies most closely associated with this tradition are the seventeenth century Royal Company of Archers in Scotland and, in England, the eighteenth century Woodmen of Arden.

Clout shooting by the Woodmen is at either 180 yards or 200 yards. The clout is 30 inches in diameter and sits in concentric rings marked on the grass, at radii of 1 1/2 feet (a "foot"), 3 feet (a "half-bow"), 6 feet (a "bow"), 9 feet (a "bow and a half"), and 12 feet (two bows), scoring 5, 4, 3, 2, and 1 point respectively. Hitting the clout gains 6 points.[6]

An alternative is scoring by "ends," since they shoot in two directions, each one being an "end," and a system similar to that used at roving is used.[7] Groups of archers shoot two arrows each, one archer at a time; he whose arrow is nearest the clout takes the point. The clout target used by the Woodmen of Arden has a hook placed centrally on both front and back on which to attach a tape measure to check distances from the clout of competing shafts. Traditionally seven points wins the game.

A marker with a small white flag is employed by the Woodmen to indicate the fall of the arrow. This he does with a complex set of maneuvers, including raising his hat and falling on his back when the clout is hit—a circumstance triggering an anxious moment by the shooter until he rises once more! Arrows nearly touching the clout are signaled by raising the hands with opposing thumbs touching, a signal known as "thumbs."[8]

A pleasant tradition involves the presence of a bottle of port behind the target, enabling those shooting to fortify themselves during an exhausting afternoon.

Marking for clout shooting embodies an element of risk, for the flight of an arrow is not always easily seen and those marking are vulnerable. Following an incident when an unfortunate marker was wounded and temporarily hospitalized, wooden pavises were made for shelter. It is recorded that with blood flow staunched and wound duly bandaged the faithful servant returned to the field to continue his marking duties.

In modern times clout shooting is a staple of the British Longbow Society, regulating body for traditional target and clout shooting in Britain. The clout itself is a white circular target of 30 inches in diameter with a 4-inch diameter central black spot. This target is set on the ground and inclined at an angle of 45 degrees. Concentric circles with 30 inch radii at four, seven, ten and thirteen feet surround it, valued respectively, 5, 4, 3, 2, and 1 point. A hit on the clout having a value of 6 points; and one cutting a circle scores the higher value. Two rounds are shot in sequence, each of thirty-six arrows shot in twelve ends of three arrows each, and in two directions.[9]

Grounds of the Royal Toxophilite Society in the mid-nineteenth century. Note the layout of the butts. (*Author*)

Next to be mentioned is shooting at butts. A formalized arrangement based loosely upon English medieval practice for warfare. Although no longer practiced, during the nineteenth century it was the favored form of social shooting.

The butt itself was made from long strips of turf pressed tightly down upon each other and was about eight feet wide, by four feet deep, by seven feet in height, becoming narrower towards the top—which was often decorated with an urn or whatever fancy the maker took.

In ancient times, when butts were erected in fields where sheep grazed, it was apparently necessary to fence them in to prevent the animals from rubbing themselves against the turf and damaging it.

Butt shooting was conducted at four distances, each a multiple of the 7 1/2 yard "rood" thus: 120 yards, 90, 60 and 30 yards. The two farthest were erected exactly opposite each other; the remainder were placed in such a position as to enable sight of the next in line when shooting. From this we probably get our word "round" since the archers shot "around" the laid out field, ending where they had started.

The target affixed to each butt was a round piece of pasteboard fastened by a peg or prick through its center. The diameter of this target varied with the distance to be shot; and since measurement was in roods, at 120 yards or 16 roods, the diameter was 16 inches, at 90 yards or 12 roods it was 12 inches, at 60 yards (8 roods) it was 8 inches, while at 30 yards (4 roods) it was just 4 inches.

Only hits within the pasteboard counted, and he (or she) with the most hits during the round won the day. Equal hits required a "shoot-off" unless account had been taken of the relative nearness of each to the peg as the round progressed.

Before leaving butts we should remember the misfortune of a certain sixteenth-century champion archer from Malling in Kent, who was so successful when shooting at them, gaining 2 or 3 shillings a day, that his fellows had him charged with witchcraft and he was severely punished.

Target shooting as we know it today had its origins in the seventeenth century when concentric circles, each with a value, were introduced. It is believed that the Society of Finsbury Archers were the innovators of this form of shooting which they regularly practiced.

The target presented to the Finsbury Archers in 1672 by their two stewards was evidently innovative, and almost certainly comprised concentric circles, but, on what it was formed is a mystery. How frustrating it is not to know. However, portable targets of oilcloth on pasteboard were the order of the day at many eighteenth century bow-meetings and speculatively the origin of these was in the previous century.

Of the targets shot yearly, that at "eleven score" was perhaps the most significant. The target itself, together with a portable "butt"—perhaps a form of target stand—was designed and presented by the aforementioned stewards for the year 1671, James Hicks and Edward Gould, and was an immediate success. It was erected yearly on the New Artillery Ground under the auspices of the Honourable Artillery Company. The eleven-score target was a costly event; those entering paid twenty shillings for the privilege; it continued, seemingly in unbroken succession, for over seventy-five years, until the last recorded shoot in 1752.

Although no doubt the members of this society met at other times and shot informally together, there were other formal

meetings regularly recorded. These were named, rather curiously, after the fees members paid to shoot. Thus they had the ten
shilling target, the five shilling target, the two shilling target, and
the six penny target. Shooting at these was competitive and for
money; the amount collected from members was distributed on
the basis of hits in particular target rings on a sliding scale. It was
therefore possible for a good archer to recoup more than he paid
to take part, and some regularly did so.

Shooting for coin persisted into the late eighteenth century,
and was adopted with enthusiasm by the Toxophilites. So enthu-
siastic were they and so improved was their shooting that the
society's treasury suffered, and in 1792 the committee put a stop
to the practice, introducing scoring as the default arrangement.
Their patron, the Prince Regent, having consolidated target circle values at 9, 7, 5, 3, and 1 for those members shooting for his
bugle prize, these were adopted by the society and eventually by
virtually everybody else, although for a time one or two individualists among the clubs remained faithful to their particular values.[11]

The matter of the value of the rings, although satisfactory to
most, offended the mathematical exactness of others, notably
young Thomas Waring who offered a plausible if convoluted
explanation of why they were all wrong.

His reasons, argued within his *Treatise on Archery*, are based
upon the relative areas occupied by the rings and their relation
to one another. We will look briefly at his findings.[12]

With each circle becoming smaller in circumference as they
approach the center it follows that the chance of hitting them
decreases. This chance is defined by value and as we know, at
present they are 1, 3, 5, 7, and 9. But, said Waring, this significantly over-rates their relative values. The real values are, from the
center outwards: gold=9; red=3; blue (inner white)=2; black=1
1/4 (or five for every four hits); and outer white=1.

This revolutionary assumption was based upon a division of
the total square inches of the four-foot circle: 1754 square inches. The five circles share this figure as follows: gold=72; red=214;
blue=352; black=490; white=626. If the aggregate amount of

every circle is divided by its width, 4 3/4 inches, the circumference of each will be: gold 15 inches; red 45 inches; blue 74 inches; black 109; and white 132.

By proportion the gold is a ninth part of the size of the white, the red is a third, the blue half, and the black four fifths. Waring elaborated on this and showed—at least to his own satisfaction—that this revision of the values was numerically sound.

The Toxophilite Society however had little desire to substitute these complex calculations for those preferred by their illustrious patron, and after acknowledging Mr. Waring's inventive argument for change consigned it to oblivion.

The Prince Regent took a practical interest in archery, and the part he played in rationalizing the distances shot today at target rounds is not always given the credit it deserves. The origin of our national men's round can be traced to that shot by the Toxophilites for silver bugles presented annually by him. It was he who stipulated that shooting should be at 100, 80, and 60 yards; although he left the matter of the number of arrows to be shot at each distance to the organizers of the meeting and these varied year by year.

It is unclear just when the straw target boss so familiar today came into being. There is circumstantial evidence for these at the national meeting held at Blackheath in 1790, since in May of that year there is reference to the sewing on of targets, speculatively to straw. Mosely, in his Essay of 1792 remarks that: "straw targets are at present more in fashion, they possess an advantage as they can be moved with ease to any destination. Their manufacture is similar to that of the common straw beehives and they are usually of four feet and one half in diameter." He goes on to mention that, "the butts used by the Royal Company of Archers at Edinburgh are made to a different principle. They too are of straw, but laid endways, and pressed down by a screw. The front is cut with a knife to provide an even surface."

Although the number of concentric rings on targets had generally stabilized at five by the end of the eighteenth century there were still those individualists whose personal preferences differed. Thus in 1791, Sir Joseph Banks, a prominent supporter of archery, ordered two targets, one of 4-feet 3-inches in diameter having five circles: a center colored gold, then three of red, finishing with an outer black. The other target was 3-feet 3-inches in diameter and had just three circles with no mention of color or of a central gold.

Personal preference was still reflected in 1793 by the Cheshire Archers with their colorful choice—a small central circle of gold leaf followed by five concentric circles of black, red, white, green and yellow.

Until well into the nineteenth century target diameters varied with the distances shot. Thus for 100 yards, a 4-foot target; for 80 yards, 3-foot; and at 60 yards, a 2-foot target. Later in this chapter we will look at the development of the target round and the emergence of competition as an ethic; but for the moment let us briefly consider a form of archery endemic to Belgium and France, although not mainstream in either Britain or the U.S.A.—I refer to the popinjay, or in continental parlance, *tir a la perche*. In its home countries it is shot by members of venerable societies whose rules and stringent regulations reflect centuries of past practice. A tall mast, up to 35 meters high, carries three or four projecting arms on which sit a number of wooden dowels fashioned after the style of a chess-set pawn and called "chicks." A larger version with feathers inserted, called the "cock bird," sits atop the mast. Arrows with special blunt ends are used, and the game is to knock down the birds, points being awarded accordingly. *Tir a la Perche* was at one time a modern Olympic event.[13]

Popinjay shooting has never been an attraction in England, although from time to time masts have been raised. A meeting in 1792 at which members of Robin Hood's Bowmen, the Woodmen of Arden, and the Toxophilites gathered to shoot in the "Flemish" style began by shooting "blazons," square targets covered by painted canvas, intersected by lines, making fifty small squares, each marked either blank or "prize." When all prizes had been won, attention turned to a mast 140 feet high on which was placed an eagle figure. After an hour of shooting, a Mr. Peacock from Robin Hood's Bowmen shot the eagle off its perch. Surely the first and only time a peacock has had the better of an eagle!

Although an activity of no great interest in England, matters are rather different in Scotland—home to shooting the papingo (Scots for popinjay), an event which the Ancient Society of Kilwinning Archers has made their own. The shoot takes place annually on the first Saturday in June at the clock tower within the grounds of the old Abbey, and the "bird"—a replica dove—is set at the height of 100 feet. Principal award is the Kilwinning Silver Arrow, a magnificent object dating from 1724 and now loaded with medallions bearing the names of past winners.

Rosettes are awarded to an archer for a shot knocking off a wing, while for the dislodging of the body his name is added to those on the Silver Arrow. In earlier days there were three elements to the Kilwinning Society—those of the gentlemen, the tradesmen, and the "callans" (juvenile boys), each distinguishable by their clothing and headgear. Now, in this egalitarian age, just a single group survives.

As the nineteenth century advanced, butt shooting remained popular among clubs with suitable facilities; however, target archery using straw bosses was fast becoming the norm and inter-club competitions began to be held.

With the onset of the Napoleonic War, the successful eighteenth-century national competitions ceased and were not resumed when life returned to normal. The wish to compete, however, was still uppermost in the minds of those with influence and, in July 1844, on the instigation of members of the Thirsk Bowmen, a meeting to discuss potential arrangements for a national meeting was held at the Black Swan hotel in York.

Reaction from clubs and their members was favorable and arrangements were made for two days shooting at Knavesmire race course, commencing on August 1—a day which dawned damp and soggy with threat of rain. Given the inclement weather a splendid total of seventy-three turned out to shoot, representative of many English and Scottish clubs. In the event, poor weather meant that the decision was made to have just one round shot over two days rather than one each day as has been done up to the present. Scores were unremarkable but all seem to have finished the rounds. One hardy fellow shot for two days and scored just 8 points for which he was awarded the wooden spoon.

The round shot was that in regular use by the West Berks Archers: six dozen arrows at 100 yards, four dozen at 80 yards, and two dozen at 60 yards. In traditional archery we know it today as the Gentlemen's National "York" Round. An important decision taken at this meeting, and one that affected clubs, was the substitution of the color blue for the inner white target ring to avoid misunderstanding by those recording hits. It is thought by some that the original color scheme reflected the heraldic requirement that a color should not be placed upon a color nor a metal on a metal, white in this case representing silver.

Markers were employed to record scores which they were forbidden to disclose; as far as it was possible, everything was arranged with typical Victorian thoroughness. Competitors shot their three arrows individually in silence, although the military band of a Regiment of Carabinieres provided stimulating music as the recording of scores took place.

Scores were not particularly exciting at this first meeting—with a potential maximum of 1440, just 221 points made Rev. Higginson the winner, for which modest result he received a vase valued at the considerable sum of £55.[14]

The meeting was considered successful and it was agreed to hold another in 1845. This too proved attractive, prompting a third; and so the sequence of annual national meetings began. Although the shoot itself was a two-day affair there was some experiment with a third day, more light hearted in nature, and in 1845 this took the form of a contest at popinjay. It was not to the liking of the competitors however and was not repeated.

Some years passed before women archers competed at national level, but after various distances and arrow numbers had been tried in 1847 and 1848, the ladies national round was finally established as four dozen arrows at 60 yards and two dozen at 50 yards and first shot in 1849.[15]

Recording of scores was diverse; if there were "score cards" or "tablets" in use in the early eighteenth century or earlier still, then to the writer's knowledge none has survived. Pens with metal nibs were available during the eighteenth century and it is speculative that these were used initially to mark hits for a more permanent record later. It is equally possible that the system of pricking hits on a card originated earlier than at present thought.

Pricking was a satisfactory and simple method whose only draw-back was a careless or inaccurate hole. Pencil marks could be excised, ink could be crossed out, but a hole was there to stay. The "pricker" was an ivory stick with a pin point; the card was rectangular in shape with lines drawn appropriate to colors and dozens shot. The system proved satisfactory and remained in use until replaced by the innovative score book and pencil—originally an ivory stick with a tapered point of lead attached, or a fountain pen.

Mild concern rumbled on across the years about the reflective effect of sunlight on the gold leaf used in the centre; and matters came to a head when, in 1884, respected Toxophilite, Mr. C. J. Longman, designed a new target face, introducing it to skeptical fellow members of the Royal Toxophilite Society. The Longman target was pale French grey color overall with a central black circle. The innovation was not well received; and after some testy correspondence in *The Field* newspaper, where it was observed that in foggy weather the target face disappeared from view, this Longman initiative was consigned to oblivion. The matter of the glinting gold was however dealt with later by the decision that in future matt paint and not gold leaf should be used.

Seldom mentioned, and not universally appreciated in earlier days were "arrow boys," those lads, often from archer families, whose dreary task it was to collect stray arrows and return them to their owners, to avoid crinoline clad ladies bending over to display an ankle—or even their under garments—and portly gentlemen from splitting their trousers.[16] It is perhaps fitting that we should end this chapter by acknowledging the benefit of their necessary presence before moving to the next, where the practical aspects of modern longbow shooting will be considered.

SEVEN

A Matter of Style

"If a mans minde fayle him, the bodye, whiche is ruled by the minde, can never do hys dutie"—Roger Ascham, 1544

What has examination of past practices and advice taught us? Can archers of today learn anything from a time when every male from seven to seventy was an archer? Did they know things that we do not? It is sometimes extremely difficult to establish exactly what these early writers meant; and trying to execute the action described in more recent booklets can result in some very strange contortions.

It is safe to say that—as today—there would have been a wide range of skills, from brilliant to buffoon. Indeed one muster of the sixteenth century[1] speaks specifically of "archers of the best sort" and of the "second sort." Presumably the also-rans were of the third sort. We know there were those who were deadly accurate—the snipers of their day—witness the tale of the Forest of Dean archer who, from the wood, sent an arrow winging into the visor of Lord Lisle at Nibley Green.[2] We know from reports of early competitions that some archers at least could loft a heavy battle shaft a considerable distance. Training from an early age was considered crucial—if for no other reason than that it built up the necessary muscles. However, in 1549, Bishop Latimer[3] considered that men would never shoot well unless they were brought up in it; while Roger Ascham, in the same decade, declared that it was far easier to teach a child the right way from the beginning than for an older archer to unlearn bad habits acquired for lack of good teaching.[4] Nowadays folk take up archery at almost any age and can still do well.

Through the centuries style has changed, influenced by the purpose for the use of the bow; but the core and essence of the advice have changed little.

One key point is that the action should be "comely" or "easy and relaxed;" and it is true that if any action, particularly in sport, looks good and appears easy then the proponent is almost certainly doing well. If the action seems awkward and ungainly then it is likely that the results are also poor.

Nevertheless, there is a qualification. You will hear it said that if you perform an action exactly the same, over and over again, then the result will be the same—which is very true. Even someone who appears awkward, if they do the same thing consistently, will find his arrows grouping. So should this matter? Is there room for individuality?

The answer is yes and no. A good coach will take into account a person's physique, and teach accordingly. However, unless certain basic rules are followed, there is a strong likelihood of both present and future damage, and the loss of vital control.

The act of shooting in a bow—any bow—requires three things of the archer if it is to be done effectively, without undue strain and/or the possibility of physical damage. These fundamentals have not changed since the first bow was invented: good, appropriate posture; correct muscle usage; and suitable rhythm.

The act of shooting accurately requires, in addition: consistency; control; and concentration.

Although these requirements are listed separately, the two groups are very closely interrelated and largely dependant upon each other.

Whether shooting target, field, clout, flight, popinjay or rovers, these requirements remain the same. Whether the bow is

A composite of the several faults usually displayed by the untutored beginner: A fistful of string; low drawing elbow; lifted front shoulder; head drawn down; bow arm rigid, with elbow in the way of the string. (*Elisabeth Allen*)

an American flatbow (AFB), a traditional longbow, a recurve, or a compound, once again the requirements are the same.

It is in the technique employed for the various disciplines that the differences lay—giving rise to the coach's assertion that "you coach the archer not the bow."

Many archers stick to one discipline, they are content, and they never have the urge to move to another. Many move happily between different forms and adjust easily. Some find this not so easy, however, so it may be helpful as we go along, to examine where differences occur and how they affect the action.

POSTURE

This is not only where your feet are, and the inclination of your body, but also your head position and the contact or reference point between drawing hand and face. This last is closely tied into consistency, since a reference point which is a "movable feast" will seriously affect accuracy. You will notice that I say reference point, not anchor point, as it used to be called—and still is by some. Anchor implies a solid unmoving "stop." In the not-so-distant-past when I first took up archery it was the norm to get the archer to come to full draw, "anchor" firmly and then start to use the back muscles to complete the shot—a double action if you like. Nowadays, although the observer may not notice it, there is a dynamic continuation of the draw right through to the release.

The importance of posture lies in the fact that good posture allows all the right muscles to work most effectively. It is also connected with the ability to aim consistently and accurately.

Ascham speaks with scorn of the many strange attitudes adopted by some archers.[5]

Thomas Waring, advising the young archer,[6] recounts that an opera dancer, Madam Bola, was entranced by what she considered a most delightful "attitude."

Alice Legh thought it an excellent fact that in shooting a young lady "*must* stand upright."[7]

The target archer, facing the same target for each shot and a (usually) level field with no obstructions, can adopt an upright stance. The position of his feet can even be marked for consistency once the optimum placing has been established. Let us pause here for a moment and observe an average archer before a shoot. He stands astride the line, raises his arms to the side, looks over his bow arm, moves it a bit, then bends down and places foot markers in the ground at his toes. What is wrong with that, you may ask.

Many folk realize that the human body is not entirely equal, with slight differences on each side. To allow for this, the archer is advised to stand across the shooting line, head slightly bowed, raise his arms to the side, lift his head and, *without moving his arms,* notice where he is actually pointing with reference to the target. Although his feet may appear in line, his body may not be and an adjustment of the feet is required so that one or the other foot is slightly behind the other. The reason for this is that when shooting, if the body itself is not aligned, the necessity to keep on aim requires a small but appreciable pressure to the side, which can affect the shot at the moment of release and produce unwanted strain. There was for a while a fashion among some archers to place their feet in such a way that they were obliged to deliberately twist the body in order to line up their shot with the target; and they firmly believed that this gave them a stronger, more immoveable stance, especially in a high wind.

The field archer, unlike the target archer, will be constantly adapting his or her stance in order to find a secure footing to

Field style. Bow and body canted. Side of face draw. Three fingers below arrow, arrow nock close to eye. (*Elisabeth Allen*)

form a good base for the shot. This may of necessity involve standing with one foot on a molehill and the other in a rabbit hole—metaphorically speaking. To enable a clear view the field archer may also need to kneel on one knee. It is often found that inclining the body will be required for a better view, or for stability, or—the least understood reason—to match the inclination of the bow. This last is particularly relevant to the traditional longbow, since clearance of the bow limbs in wooded areas, plus an arrow flight which passes cleanly through vegetation and branches, often requires inclination—or canting—of the bow.

Whatever the stance and whatever the body inclination, the key to control will still be in maintaining the line up between bow hand, arrow nock, and drawing elbow—known as the draw force line.

The field archer will be dealing with shots at differing distances but they will all be shorter than the 100 yards of the York round. For this reason—if he is shooting instinctively—he will generally bring his drawing hand up the side of his face, making the distance between the arrow nock and his aiming eye a very close one and enabling either a good instinctive shot, or a conscious point of aim.

However, by lifting the rear of the arrow, the front is effectively lowered—no problem at short range, but a good deal of ground will be lost; which is why the target archer is advised to keep the drawing hand below his chin for maximum distance.

Moving the drawing hand up the side of the face can produce another effect that must be allowed for. The arrow nock will no longer be directly under the aiming eye unless the head is adjusted accordingly. Thus your field archer will not only be canting the bow but his whole upper body and head will follow this line up.

It was Horace Ford who first put into writing the fact that accurate aiming required the arrow to be directly beneath the aiming eye—and after his instructive book[8] was published scores rose quite dramatically. However, some archers with a shorter forearm may not be able to establish a good line unless their drawing hand moves from front of face to slightly at the side.

Our target archer, standing upright but relaxed, and bringing his drawing hand under his chin, still needs to ensure that his aiming eye is directly over the arrow, and this demands a certain head position. If his forearm length is such that he can keep a good straight draw force line with the string coming to the center of his nose and chin, then his head will need to tilt not toward the hand but away from it. If, however, his arm length requires that his hand move further back alongside his face, then a more upright head position will bring the eye over the arrow nock. We shall return to the matter of arm length and reference point later.

As a target archer shooting a full competitive round, the requirement is to perform one perfect shot and 143 action replays. An archer who is purely instinctive will find this hard, because, although the first shot may be fine, the second and third may be less so, for the application of instinctive shooting is where each shot is different and performed without consciously aiming. Asked to repeat it, the genuinely instinctive archer can find it extremely difficult if not impossible.

In other types of shooting it can be seen that the principles of correct posture must still be adhered to in order to ensure that muscles can work most effectively and aiming is accurate.

Clout, roving, and particularly flight shooting, demand an ability to send the arrow farther than either field or target. The

Clout style. Maintaining the draw force line while aiming high for distance. (*Elisabeth Allen*)

tendency here is for the archer to raise his bow arm, since he will be aiming into the sky in order to achieve the distance required. Even Ford speaks of raising the bow arm,[9] and it is far from clear whether he really did mean just that arm. However, this action will not only shorten the draw length—resulting in a loss of distance—but also put the shoulder girdle out of alignment, so that the bow drawing action is no longer taking place in the most efficient way. Tackling the requirements of long distance shooting needs to be done with what is known as unit aiming, in which the legs and hips remain still, but the upper body tilts backwards as one unit, thus keeping the draw force line exactly the same as it would be when shooting at the targets.

The only exception to this is for those engaged in shooting the replica war bow, where it is common to see the archer bend his rear knee as he leans back into what will be a dynamic shot. You will also find some clout archers using this method, especially if they find it difficult to bend their upper body sufficiently.

MUSCLE USAGE

It may be stating the obvious, but if the body is correctly aligned then there is a fair chance that the right muscles will come into play; and this is a component of control. If the wrong muscles are used, then after a while they begin to tire and the archer is no longer fully in control of his equipment or of the shot. In such circumstances one will often see trembling at full draw, a snap release or a forward loose that does not send the arrow where it is meant to go.

It is fair to say that the archer who is most likely to walk away with the trophy is the one who at the end of the day still looks the same for the last few shots as he did for the first ones. Sadly, it is also common to see, along the shooting line, archers who are struggling to come to full draw or (for the recurve shooter) to get through the clicker.

Quite a few men are capable of "muscling through" a bow on their arms for a while, but very few indeed can keep this up for a whole day's shooting.

As most coaches will tell you, it is sometimes difficult to persuade an archer to use a bow within his capabilities. If you are facing the French, with your 30-inch heavyweight arrows, then the training you received since childhood will have built up your muscles to the extent that you can deal with a powerful bow. And a powerful bow will indeed be required to loft the arrow as far as possible into the advancing army. You will most likely only get the chance to get away half a dozen shots before the enemy is too close and hand-to-hand fighting begins.

On the local archery field with a target no more than 100 yards away, and light target arrows, combined with the fact that you need to shoot 144 of them, you will struggle for control if your bow is too powerful. The message is that the wise archer uses a bow that is right for the job. Having said that, it is perfectly possible to train up muscles to the extent that you can control a powerful bow; members of various war-bow groups do just that.

The target archer needs sufficient power in his bow to give a reasonable aim at 100 yards. The field archer looks for a flat trajectory to provide clearance in wooded areas and allow for ground lost from the use of a high side of face reference point, and will choose a stronger bow, but the number of times he uses it and the rests in between make this more practical.

Without the benefit of recurved limbs and modern materials, the traditional longbow archer will need a bow which is a little

Joseph Gibbs, member of the English War Bow Society, getting his whole body into a dynamic draw. (*Author*)

stronger than the average modern target bow. Generally a compromise is necessary between a good point of aim with a flat trajectory and a bow which can be handled all day without tiring. The inevitable result of using inappropriate muscles is that they tire more quickly and begin to offload onto other muscles. At the least this can mean loss of the all important control, at the worst it could cause damage.

The admonition to "get it on your back" is almost as old as archery. In a sermon given before Edward VI in 1549, Bishop Latimer bewailed the fact that the nation's shooting had declined and men were less able to use the really strong bows.[10]

The bowman of old—as Latimer remarked—did indeed lay his body in the bow, as he drew much farther than our target or field archers do today. If you watch those who shoot the heavy or war bow you will observe much the same thing as they go for the maximum they can get out of their bows. One is reminded of the sheriff's admonition to Robin Hood to "pull it to thine ear."[11]

Whereas much has been said about the use of the back, there was, until recently, a dearth of those capable of explaining *how* to do this.

Nowadays there should not be any coach with a current ticket who is unable to assist the archer in getting this action performed correctly; while it is relatively simple to talk an aspiring archer through an exercise or movement which clearly illustrates what it feels like when the back is working properly. The use of an elbow cup is particularly useful in this respect, since it forces the archer to use those muscles which draw back the elbow, rather than allowing the fingers, forearm or bicep to pull back the string.

To explain in writing is rather more difficult, like trying to describe a spiral staircase without using your hands. Imagine if you will an archer at full draw and the forces in play. The bow is continuously trying to fold him up; but to counteract this he has across his back a sort of powerful elastic "rope" which will take the strain. The only way this will work effectively, however, is if his shoulders are down and relaxed, not hunched up, and his drawing arm elbow is level. This last is important and—as mentioned above—is influenced by the length of the forearm and the point of reference.

To illustrate this, a personal anecdote: For many years I shot well—to what was then Master Bowman standard, but was aware that my drawing elbow was higher than it should be and my wrist had a distinct kink upwards. I had been taught to bring the string to the center of my nose and chin, in the style favored at the time. Eventually I reached the point where I could not shoot for the pain in my distorted wrist. A coach, attempting to correct my elbow position insisted that of course I could get my elbow down, and attempted to do so by physically pushing it. Needless to say this was painful and did not have the desired result. It was not until I moved my point of reference back slightly to the side of my face that my elbow came down quite easily. I did have to learn a new head position, but from then on my draw force line was as it should be.

Let me offer an exercise that will make this clear.

Left, a front of face draw with short fore arm, resulting in a high drawing elbow and third finger hardly on the string. Right, moving to a side of face draw enables the drawing elbow to come into proper alignment for a good draw-force-line and a longer draw length. (*Elisabeth Allen*)

Stand as if about to shoot and place the back of your bow hand on the shoulder blade of your drawing arm, so that you can feel what that shoulder is doing. Turn your head as if shooting and bring your drawing arm up until the hand is at your normal reference point. A mirror will help here as you notice whether your arm is level. If it is, then—maintaining the finger/jaw contact—move your elbow backwards as if you are pulling the bow and feel what your shoulder blade is doing. Now return to the start position, deliberately lift your elbow and again move it backwards. You should find that with the elbow raised the shoulder blade moves very little or not at all.

When you begin this exercise, if you find that your elbow is already high, move your hand back a little along the side of your face, remembering to keep your hand under your chin, until you can level the arm and at once you will find that you can move the elbow back as if pulling and the shoulder will do its work. This is an indication that you should be seriously considering a new reference point. It does not need to be all that much further back, but will allow your arm to assume a more level position and the shoulder to work as it should.

"But how will I make sure I come to the same place each time?" you may ask. It is easy to find a central front of face point, not so easy at the side. Some archers seek the answer to a consistent reference point in the use of a platform tab—and these are not banned by the British Longbow Society. Used correctly they can be helpful; but there is a very strong tendency for the platform tab to tilt up along the jaw-line, and almost immediately the drawing elbow rises. So use such a tab with great caution. What you can do—and still within the society rules—is use a "kisser" on the string. There are little plastic commercial kissers, or you can make your own with some thread and glue. All you need is to produce a small lump on the string which—when you draw—arrives at the corner of your mouth if you are drawing to the side of your face, or the center of your lips if you are drawing to the front. Make sure it is set on the string so that your hand lies neatly beneath your chin.

Once your bow is in your hand, remember to execute the pulling action by pressing the elbow back around behind you, letting the action between string and elbow "stretch" the forearm and especially the fingers, back of hand and wrist. Unwanted tension in the hand should disappear and the whole arm will be more relaxed. I know of some coaches who give their pupils a well-weighted bag to hold down by their side, and encourage them to let it literally hang on the fingers, and this can work well. It also can help with learning to loose effectively as we shall see.

Check your progress by using an elbow cup which enables you to pull your bow without having the string on the fingers. If the feeling is different when shooting, then you are not using the right muscles and more practice with the elbow cup is required.

Having got the back working well, what about the front arm? There is a tendency among new archers toward the idea that the arm which holds the bow must be tensed, jammed out firmly like a rod of iron, solid and stable. This was certainly advocated by some of the experts of old; and the idea frequently lives on in the minds of more established archers, although it may have gone underground into the unconscious.

Some will ask "How else am I to stop the bow from folding me up?" The answer is the correct positioning of the bones into a supportive prop.

Those offering advice in the past—as we have seen—have varied widely in their suggestions, some even advocating turning the arm/wrist in—this is not recommended. One thing almost universally mentioned by non-archers who have briefly experienced the use of the bow is, "I had a go once—I got an awful bruise where I hit my arm." A beginner who is found shooting with a very bent elbow—or a very long bracer—has almost certainly hit his arm at some time. So—what to do? If the bow arm is lifted to the shooting position and the arm then completely bent at the elbow, the movement should be horizontal; if it is vertical the elbow is not turned as it should be.

The two bones in our forearm enable us to turn our hands palm up or palm down, with the bones crossing to allow this. What is required here is to keep the hand still and turn the other end of the bones so that the elbow is pointing horizontally. This can be practiced by holding the edge of an open door to keep the hand still and "rolling" the elbow back and forth until it becomes second nature. It will be found that, even with the elbow rolled into the horizontal, the bones of the arm can still be lined up in such a way that the pressure of the bow handle passes along those bones and into the shoulder which should be settled down—the prop as mentioned above.

Advice on the position of the hand itself has varied with different writers. Because a longbow handle is straight and not shaped, as is a modern target bow, closing the hand around it will mean the wrist will be somewhat down. Those shooting the modern recurved bow are recommended to maintain a light hold, with the hand at around 45 degrees, but a wrist strap is usually employed to stop the bow falling when the string is released. However, it is perfectly possible to use a similar, relaxed hold on a longbow, with the hand slightly angled, as long as there is enough finger and thumb curve around the handle to prevent it falling. The main considerations are—what is comfortable and what will not have a bad effect upon the bow at the loose. Imagine an invisible line from your hand to the aiming point, with the bow pressing into the thumb joint. What happens at the loose we will see in a moment.

So now it is clear what stance is most beneficial; the next question is how to get there. Placing the arrow on the string may be accomplished in whatever way is comfortable to the archer; and provided the "cock" feather faces out away from the bow there is little more to be said.

Writers of the past have come up with a number of different ways of holding the string, most of them would be regarded by coaches today as peculiar at least and inadvisable at best. We read of slanting fingers, of more pressure on first and third fingers, and of the string on the finger pads. Let us briefly look at why these methods have little to recommend them.

When the heavy war bow was in use, the method of drawing back the string of necessity required a good strong hold. It is thought by some that what we call the Mediterranean loose, using three fingers, had its nascence at this time, since other methods in vogue would not have allowed the archer to cope with the effort required. Despite the myth of the waving two fingers, it is unlikely that only two would have been used, without perhaps the support of the thumb. Today's warbow enthusiasts have—by request—tried using two fingers to draw their heavy bows and found it difficult and not to their liking. During the Edwardian era there were some lady archers who chose to use just first and second fingers, but their bows were comparatively light. Just two fingers certainly give less drag as the string moves forward. However, the accepted method today for target archery requires three, one above and two below the arrow nock, whilst the field archer, bringing his hand up the side of his face, will place all three fingers below the arrow in order to get the arrow nock as close to his aiming eye as possible.

The most effective place for the string is in the first groove of the fingers—pressure here actually tends to bend the fingers slightly anyway. This position best enables the hand to relax; and when we come to releasing we shall see why this is important. Care should be taken to adjust the fingers so that all three are equally in use, although the top index finger may be allowed to be a little "lazy." This will mean that the third finger takes slightly more pressure than the other two. This position is closely tied up with the drawing elbow and whether it is level. A high elbow will mean the third finger is not sufficiently on the string.

Above all, avoid taking the string on the finger pads as so many archers did in Ford's day. This was at a time when "tips" were used and these encouraged a finger pad hold. Contrary to some archers' belief, this does not allow a better release, because there is too much strain on the ligaments required to keep the fingers bent. The hand is under stress and it cannot relax effectively at the moment of release. It is said that even the great Ford was forced to take a break from his shooting when he suffered tendon damage. So a good hook on the string is strongly recommended.

The next stage in the shot is also open to variety. Some past writers said little about how to get from the placing of the fingers on the string to what we call full draw, while others provided guidance. In truth it matters little how the archer reaches the required position provided the shoulder girdle is correctly aligned and the right muscles are being used. At the time I was first instructed, the favored method was what we have now come to refer to as the "V" draw. The archer held the bow horizontally at his side, positioned his fingers on the string and then drew both hands apart equally as he raised the bow to the shooting position.

The downside of this method is that it is too easy to also raise the shoulders at the same time, especially the bow arm shoulder, which means that the back muscles will not be performing their job correctly and the shoulder girdle will be out of alignment. Advocates of this method taught that having reached full draw the archer then tensed his back muscles during what they called the "hold;" but it is questionable whether this was the most practical or effective action.

Today the draw most favored—at least for target and clout shooting—is what is called the "T draw," whereby the archer, with fingers on string, holds the bow upright towards the target, settles his bow shoulder down and into the correct position and then employs the drawing arm shoulder to pull the arm around until the required position is achieved. If executed correctly this means that everything is correctly aligned.

When shooting clout starting with a T draw ensures that, even though the archer then leans back for elevation, the draw force line is maintained, because the aim is taken and the draw made, before he bends at the waist. Flight shooters, however, will tend to lean back to the very specific angle required for maximum distance before drawing the bow and releasing the arrow in one quick movement.

The field archer will adapt to the conditions and evolve a drawing technique that is easy to accomplish among trees and bushes.

Those shooting the heavy or war bow use a variation of the "V draw" as they often begin by bending forward with the arrow pointing towards the ground and their drawing elbow up. They then expand into the draw as they lean back, raise the bow and pull back to the ear or beyond to get the maximum out of the bow and achieve the greatest distance in a burst of power.

RHYTHM

Establishing a regular pattern and tempo influences the consistency of the shot and also has a direct connection with control.

Once an archer has moved beyond the early stages of learning, a regular rhythm will often occur naturally. It is something within the mind—almost unconscious, a sort of tick tock. What goes wrong is when the rhythm falters and one shot is held longer than another, or is rushed away. The target archer with a recurved or compound bow will almost invariably be seen to pause on aim—sometimes for what seems like quite a while. He will be working to come through a clicker so that his draw is a precise length, and if he is using the clicker correctly it will click exactly at the time when all else is right and the shot is ready to go. The longbow archer has no such constraint. He alone must decide not only that he has drawn exactly to the right length, but also that he is precisely on aim. And he must do this within a reasonably short moment. It is not advisable to hold a longbow at full draw for too long, since the bow held long will tire and slightly less power will be produced when it is released, with the result that the arrow will go a little lower. A longbow at full draw is also—to quote an old saying—nine tenths broken and it is unwise to expect it to bend for too long.

Is there advice on how long to hold? Historically, I could find none; and I doubt that the warbowman would have held for any length of time at all; the shot would have been "up and away," despite what film makers show us in such classics as *Henry V*. From personal experience and observation, I would advise that you need to hold just long enough to be certain that you have settled and stopped moving and that you are on aim; there is little if any advantage in holding longer.

Some who are aware of the fact that they should not hold too long get into the habit of snap shooting. Thus does consistency and control go out of the window. And here we need to introduce another "c"—calmness. This is control of the mind as well as the body.

It has been said that the hardest part of an archer to coach is the bit between his ears—a cliché perhaps, but nonetheless it is often very true. The longbow archer will retort, "I am there to enjoy myself. What's all this about the mental approach?" Those of old giving advice did not bother themselves too much with what went on in the archer's mind; unlike the far eastern Master who counsels the exponent of the art of archery, that one should be on good terms with everyone on their way to the shooting place. In other words, if you are in a bad temper you are not going to shoot well and you might as well go home.

And to the archer who suggests that he is there only for enjoyment, I would say that if you shoot well it is most likely that your enjoyment will increase, so anything which helps that process should not be dismissed.

As indicated, much of the necessary rhythm starts in the mind. There should be a clear feeling that the whole shot flows steadily from start to finish. This will be best accomplished if you are relaxed, so that only those muscles necessary to complete the drawing of the bow are in use. If you are a swimmer you will know well that unless you relax as you move through the water you will not progress well. In the same way, the archer must be relaxed—although not in the way one of my pupils was. I observed him standing on the line slumped like a badly packed sack of potatoes. "Well" he told me, "you said I must relax," to which I was obliged to retort, "I said relax, not collapse."

Imagine, if you like, that you are giving a demonstration of how a perfect shot is made. If my pupils find it difficult to establish a regular rhythm I generally advise that they find some phrase or melody which suits them and matches the required timing of the shot as they let the melody go through their mind. I hesitate to suggest "Nock two three, fingers two three, draw two three," for this has a dreadful feeling of regimentation about it, but you get the idea. After a while there should be no need to use the ditty, as a regular rhythm should become established and automatic. If, however, the archer's shooting deteriorates and becomes ragged, a return to the favorite ditty should get him back on track.

And then all you have to do is let go—right?

THE RELAXED LOOSE

It might surprise the reader to learn that letting the string go can create a real problem in some people's minds. In my early coaching days I was quite flummoxed—having got my beginner at full draw and having said "Now let go of the string"—when she asked, "How do I let go?" There is also the incredible but true tale of a young, fairly new, archer, helping out at a 'have-a-go,' who, with his pupil at full draw said, "Now let go" and she did—she let go of the bow.

A wise coach will have his newcomer hold the bow horizontally, with arrow pointing to the ground, then encourage him to push back his drawing elbow as he relaxes the fingers, in order to acquaint them with the correct action. Some coaches have been known to use the heavy bag method, whereby the newcomer lets the bag hang on their fingers by their side and then lets it slip off.

In Japan they speak of snow settling on a bamboo leaf until quite suddenly it dips and the snow drops—a moment which cannot be predicted. One Japanese master suggests that we observe how tightly a child will hold a proffered finger, yet how smoothly the finger is released, for the child does not think, "I will let go."[12] Not all Western archers find it easy to understand these analogies.

All this does, however, lead us to the idea that the good archer does not "let go" of the string but rather *stops holding* it or *allows it to go,* by totally relaxing his fingers. Human fingers—I am told—just cannot move fast enough to get out of the way of a bowstring which is trying to move forward; so the fingers must relax and allow the string to flip them out of the way. Simple.

Ok, keep working on it.

By way of further explanation, I have seen an extreme slow motion video of a top archer releasing, and it really does look as if the string has gone through her fingers, for they are still so relaxed. Equally I have seen archers who—having been told that when they release the string their hand should move backwards—open their fingers, the arrow flies off and *then* they move their hand back to their shoulder. A clear misunderstanding of the concept of the follow through.

Perhaps here we need a little about the follow through and how/why it happens. If our archer thinks about a golfer hitting the ball, a footballer kicking, a tennis player returning the ball over the net, there is something they all have in common. The action does not stop dead at the moment of impact but continues in the same direction. An archer is not hitting anything but there is a line of force which we have previously noted, with a momentary balance at full draw between the effort he is making to hold back the string and the pull of the bow limbs. At the moment of relaxing the fingers, the pull of the bow vanishes, but the effort of pressing back the drawing elbow continues for a moment and so the arm slips backwards in a natural reflex. If all the right muscles are in use there is no need to manufacture a follow through—it will happen quite naturally. I often place my hand on the back of a pupil's drawing elbow and encourage them to push it out of the way as they release the string and this usually has the desired effect.

Why is the follow through important? It is a sign that the draw force line is correctly established, it maintains the necessary position of the upper body in relation to the target, so that there is no adverse affect on the passage of the arrow, and it will also prevent what is called the 'fly away' loose which will send the arrow off its desired path.

That is the 'back' end; so what happens at the front? The hand is propping the bow in place and at the moment of release there should be a slight push of the bow directly towards the target. Imagine if you will that there is a string connecting the bow handle with the point of aim and that, as you loose, the string is tugged slightly. This too maintains a line of effort that will send the arrow where it should go. A good follow through prevents that action which may often be seen on the shooting line, when the archer "explodes" in what seems like all directions, bow going one way, drawing arm the other. This can adversely influence the arrow direction; and to reinforce a good follow through I often suggest that my pupil continues to aim until the arrow hits the target—once again we find advice in the past which told us the same thing.

AIMING

We have previously mentioned the archer who 'snaps' shoots, as a result of worrying about holding the bow too long. There is, though, another reason, which is rather more disquieting, and which has affected a very large number of archers over the years, causing them a great deal of concern. Equally, much has been written about how to overcome this phenomenon. It has several names and you will be familiar with at least one of them: Target panic, target shyness, the "doom," gold shy.

For those fortunate enough never to have experienced target shyness, a short explanation. The archer goes through the usual sequence, comes to full draw and finds either that he cannot bring the sight onto the gold (if he is using a sight) or he cannot let go or he lets go too soon, or when he is not "on aim." A longbow archer will of course not have a sight; but it is not uncommon to see a shot released when it is clear that the archer was not on aim, or had not settled or was not ready. There are two main reasons for this. One is lack of control—usually caused by trying to use weak muscles that are not up to the task; the other is a concern—often unconscious—about where the arrow will go. When it really matters that the next arrow is in the gold then control can evaporate. Once this problem starts it is self-perpetuating so it is imperative that it is dealt with.

Historically target panic does not seem to figure in the writing of those giving advice. We have no way of knowing whether or not it was a feature of early archery. More recently, various suggestions have been offered, the most radical of which is to change hands and shoot the other way around. This did, I believe, work for at least some archers.

Before looking more closely at this phenomenon and how it can be corrected, it might perhaps be pertinent to talk a little about aiming.

Ascham does not mention aiming as part of the recommended sequence, only "holding," and says little else about it other than to advise the archer not to look at the arrow but to look at the mark. He seemed not to favor aiming as we would understand it—which seems quite incredible to modern thought. If we want to hit something surely we must aim at it? What Ascham was concerned with was "keeping a line" and "keeping a length"—in other words maintaining a direct line with the mark and maintaining a consistent elevation. When looked at in relation to our modern archer, there is actually little with which to disagree.

Very little else can be gleaned about aiming from other historic advice, until we come to the great Horace Ford, whose intricate examination of the whole act of shooting had such a remarkable effect not only on his own generation of archers but on many to follow.

He it was who—remarking that if one aims a gun then the sight is lined up with the target by placing the eye directly behind it—reasoned that the same idea held good for archery. Such a simple point, but until then not a major part of the archery scene, as most people drew to the side of the face and, presumably, aimed off to compensate—or missed.

It is an exceedingly lucky longbow archer who finds he can aim his arrow point blank at the centre of the target from at least one of the distances at which he is required to shoot. Although the British Longbow Society does allow a mark or rubber band on the upper limb to provide a way of keeping a constant elevation, many choose not to avail themselves of this. These archers can be seen aiming by pointing their arrows at treetops, or other natural features. Ford is said to have used a window in one of the College buildings at Cheltenham. One archer of my acquaintance was heard complaining bitterly at a bow meeting, that the car in the parking lot that he was using as an aiming mark had just been driven off. Likewise, passing clouds are also not the best things to choose as a point of aim.

At the shorter distances things change, and a convenient daisy or other vegetation which lies part of the way to the target may be chosen, or—again with society approval—a marker may be placed in front of the target as an aiming mark. Newcomers are often astounded that there are distances at which it is necessary to aim well below the target. This requirement is caused by the fact that an arrow does not travel in a straight line, but in a ballistic curve, so at the shorter ranges it is still rising as it reaches the target.

It is only with experience and practice that an archer will work out where he needs to point his arrow at each distance in order to maximize his chances of hitting the target. This we call point of aim.

With the elevation (Ascham's "keeping a length") sorted, what about the line? Here again it is not always possible to line up exactly with the target—although those archers keen to do well will endeavor to match arrows with bow sufficiently well to require as little aiming off as possible. A poor loose can send the arrow off to one side, as can moving the bow hand too soon— and more of this later. But there is one simple practice that not every archer is aware of which will greatly improve the aim and—all other things being well executed— will ensure that the arrow follows the intended line.

Remembering that accuracy requires the aiming eye to be over the arrow, how can the archer be sure that it is? A simple check while at full draw will do this. If the aiming eye is correctly positioned, the archer will see the string—rather wide and out of focus—directly in front of his eye. All he needs to do is ensure that the string is lined up with the arrow point with which he is aiming. I always use the phrase "look through the string at the arrow" One more thing. If string and arrow are not lined up, the way to correct this is not to move either bow or string, but to move the head—and thus the eye—very slightly. It will be found that only a small tilt one way or the other is necessary.

Archer attempting to use left eye while shooting right-handed. (*Elisabeth Allen*)

AIMING EYE

One thing about which there is nothing at all to be gleaned from those in the past, purveying their wisdom to aspirant archers, and that is which eye should be used, since in the past it was generally reckoned that all archers shot right-handed, and would either have kept both eyes open or aimed with their right eye. In fact left-handedness was seen as something to be decried—from it we get our expression "sinister" which has now come to mean evil and menacing rather than just "left."

In particular we find that no less a person than G. A. Hansard, writing in 1841, describes a left-handed archer as "the most ungainly of monsters"[13] and there was at least one nineteenth century club which stated in its rules that no left-handed archers would be allowed on their ground.[14] Thankfully today we are rather more enlightened.

One of the first things a coach will (or should) do with a newcomer is establish which is their natural "aiming" eye. This has also been called the master eye, although I do not like this name. Basically it is the eye that the brain chooses when we need to line something up with something else. Since our two eyes provide us with binocular vision, which serves to give us the ability to gauge distances, we get a slightly different view with each eye of which we are normally unaware. Our brain then "chooses" the image from just one eye when and as required and we are totally unaware of this. If we are lucky, hand matches eye and we can even shoot with both eyes open if we wish to, which has been advocated in the past and still is today, as it eliminates the muscular stress of closing one eye.

Unfortunately, the natural aiming eye does not always match with the handedness—and there is a problem to be dealt with.

There are three camps in this regard. One states categorically that the archer *must* shoot to the aiming eye. One camp says shoot to your handedness and cover or close the aiming eye. My camp says let us find out which is more comfortable for the newcomer and work with that. Non-matching eye and hand are only a problem if they are not recognized and made allowance for. Then you will see the new archer at full draw has his head tipped over awkwardly attempting to aim with the "wrong" eye.

When first learning to shoot it is fairly easy to learn either way, but I have found some cross laterals, as they are known, who—after careful experimenting—prefer to shoot using their natural aiming eye and others who prefer to go with their handedness.

To establish which is the aiming eye there are many methods. I like to use one that allows newcomers to notice for themselves the difference. With both arms at full stretch towards the target I ask them to make a small "window" with forefingers and thumbs. Then with both eyes open to look at the gold center through the window. I then—warning them to keep quite still—bring my hand across one eye and ask, "can you still see the gold?," followed by covering the other eye and asking the same question. My pupils will immediately notice that with one eye uncovered they can see the gold and with the other it has "jumped" out of view and thus they understand the concept of the aiming eye being the one which still sees the gold. If they prove to be cross lateral I encourage them to begin by trying this new skill using their aiming eye, emphasizing that if they feel uncomfortable they will be free to change around. Some try both ways several times before coming to a decision—but it is ultimately theirs to make—and I always have an eye patch at the ready.

CONTROL

Having moved from the initial stance to the correct usage of muscles, and a good steady rhythm to the aiming, all this is of no help if the archer panics, cannot bring his aim to where he wishes, or releases the arrow too soon. Although this problem would appear to be more common amongst recurve archers using a sight which they find they are unable to line up with the Gold, I will address this anyway, for the benefit of the longbow shooter who has also experienced target shyness. Does he need to become a beginner again and learn to shoot the other way around? Not really.

I have found one simple method which does seem to work well and can be adapted for either recurve archers using a sight or longbow archers using point of aim, and I offer it here.

The afflicted archer is required to *not* shoot for some time. This does not mean packing up his bow and taking up golf. It means going to the practice ground with bow and arrows, setting up a target at fairly short range—say about ten yards—and removing the colored roundel target face.

Facing the bare boss he then goes through the actions of "setting up" a shot; but, before he does, he tells himself firmly that he is *not* going to shoot the arrow. If all goes well he will pause for a moment with the arrow pointing at the target and then will "come down" and rest.

After a moment he will go through this again, and again, until he can come to full draw, with his hand at the right reference point and back muscles taking the strain. He will concentrate on how this feels. He will concentrate on consistently arriving at the same body position. Closing his eyes can be very helpful at this stage. What he must not do is shoot any arrows.

When the archer feels that he is in control and is arriving at a good full draw position regularly, he should pack up and go home. At quiet moments, he can consolidate what he has done by mentally thinking it through, imagining himself still before the bare boss, coming to full draw, holding for a moment, and then coming down.

What I cannot tell you is how many times this needs to be done, because much depends on the individual. But when he feels that control has been established, the next step is to place an aiming mark on the boss—just a square of paper—and go through the whole exercise again. No closing of eyes this time, but learning to come on to aim, holding for a moment while maintaining control and then coming down. Once again it is up to the individual to decide he is ready for the next step. Is he completely in control? Is he coming to full draw correctly? Is the urge to release mastered? If he is confident about this then again pack up and go home.

Step three requires the archer to replace the target face and upon it place several aiming spots, randomly, which can be small pieces of paper, target pins or crosses marked on the face. The non-shooting exercise is then gone through as before, but this time the archer decides which spot he will aim at each time. This method works for longbow or barebow archers; for those using a sight the only aiming spot will be the gold. As with the other steps, the archer should stop when he is satisfied.

Ignoring the amused comments of his fellow archers when he continues to aim but not loose, his final step is to start moving the target further away, while the "hold and come down" control is maintained and each time a different aiming spot is selected. On some occasions the archer may find that he looses involuntarily, but this should be ignored and he should return to the original practice.

There will come a time—and I am afraid I cannot say when, only the archer himself will know—when he can return to normal shooting because his control is now sufficiently established. If control vanishes again then a return to non-shooting practice for a while is required

If you are still with me you may be wondering about practicing. Many archers ask how often? How many arrows? and so forth. There are two points I would make, and the first is that if you have a particular aspect of your shot which you wish to work on until you get it right, then at the point when you feel you have accomplished what you set out to do, STOP. Pack up and go home. As with the target panic exercise, you can run through your sequence at home in your mind, and this will reinforce the action.

If you feel that there is nothing specific you wish to work on but the physical act of shooting, then remember the adage that whatever you practice you make perfect and therefore if you practice a bad habit you will get very good at it. So keep your practice fairly short, making sure each shot is the best you can make it. Two-dozen arrows shot thoughtfully and with care are worth far more than twelve dozen flung down the field. If you are seeking to strengthen muscles then there are exercises that will help you do this. One obvious one is just pulling and letting down your bow—but a word of warning here. It is easy to relax your guard and go onto automatic, resulting in an unplanned release of the string—not a good idea for a longbow. Some archers, aware of this possibility, always have an arrow on the string when employing this method, and many a wardrobe has been skewered that way; but at least the energy has been dissipated and the bow not put at risk.

CALMNESS

We have already touched on the desirability of arriving at the ground in good spirits, at peace with the world. Many an archer has said, and I can vouch for this personally, that a period of shooting is of itself relaxing; troubles vanish, if only for a while, and the archer travels home in happy mood. But if he is shooting in a competition, then he is not free to allow time to relax him, he must be relaxed from the first arrow; and here careful preparation is important.

It goes without saying that equipment should all be in apple pie order and minor repairs are not left until the night before. The wise archer will also ensure that he knows exactly where the ground is and how to get there; plenty of time has been allowed for possible hold-ups and he has also run through his written checklist as the car is packed.

There is little that can be done about annoying snarl ups en route; but some deep breathing, plus whatever kind of music you find relaxing, will help.

Upon arrival find your place, and set up. Then is the time to warm up. Yes! Warm up! Gentle mobility and stretching exercises will not only prepare your muscles for their task but also relax the mind. This is, I find, the one area where many archers are lacking. It is a kindness to your body to prepare it for a day's shooting; and believe me you will shoot better for it.

Many moons ago, at a bow meeting taking place in the most appalling wind and rain, conscious of the fact that longbow archers are said to shoot for enjoyment, one soggy archer was heard to remark, "I have enjoyed about as much of this as I can stand."

May I conclude with a wish that, not withstanding the occasional upset, your longbow shooting will be a pleasant experience—which I am sure it will be, an experience which I can only encapsulate in the following, penned after a particularly uplifting day on the grounds of Bath Archers, Somerset.

Russet trees along the hill.
In the hedge a blackbird's trill.
Now and then a gentle breeze
Stirs, among the nearby trees,
Traces of the morning mist,
By the autumn sunlight kissed.

To the targets, in a row,
Gentlemen and ladies go
Costumed as in days of old
O the pleasure of a Gold!
Picture then this tranquil scene,
Red and gold and brown and green.

Once again the bows are bent,
On their way the arrows sent.
Friendly laughter on the line
"Did your arrow hit, or mine?"
Here is what's best for all to see
Union, trueheart and courtesie.*

Come, with your fellow archers stand,
A bow of yew firm in your hand.
For a while turn back the page
Remembering a more gracious age
Enjoy, in pleasant company,
This sport as it was meant to be.

Such a day will end, you'll find
In calm and happy frame of mind.
When sweetly spent the hours fly
And all too soon the day goes by.
Pack up your bow, time for some tea
And talk of days that used to be.
Though there may be no prize for me,
To share such sport, in harmony
With others of like mind and heart,
To try my skill and take my part.
Say, can there be a nicer way
To spend a golden autumn day?

*Motto of the Grand National Archery Society

Glossary

Archer's paradox. The circumstance whereby an arrow, when released does not travel along the line where it is pointing, but paradoxically flies to the target by bending around the bow limb. (Only applies to a longbow.)

Arrow pass. A position on the upper limb where the arrow is placed to be drawn. Immediately adjacent to the upper edge of the handle. On self-yew bows often identified by a mother of pearl plate, used to protect the bow.

Barbed broadhead. A wide bladed arrowhead having backward facing prongs, designed to maximise damage to flesh.

Barrelled. An arrow shaft thicker in the center and tapering to each end.

Belly wedge. A triangular wooden or cork piece mounted on the upper bow limb behind the arrow pass to prevent damage to a bow by the over-drawing of an arrow.

Birding bow. A long bow of light draw-weight suited to taking birds and small game.

Bob-tailed. An arrow shaft thicker at the head tapering to the string notch (nock),

Bough bow. A long bow constructed from the bough of a tree. Considered inferior in cast to one made from the trunk or bole.

Breasted. An arrow thicker at the nock tapering to the head.

Butt. An earth or turf mound on the face of which a target or "mark" is placed.

Carriage bow. A bow made either hinged or in two parts for ease of conveyance.

Compass. A bow is said to come in "full compass" when at full draw its curve is one complete arc.

Doubly barrelled. A "waisted" arrow shaft with two thicker parts each side of the center, which taper to nock and head.

Draw force line. An imaginary, straight line extending from the heel of the bow hand to the point of the elbow of the drawing hand when the bow is fully drawn up.

Drawing. The act of pulling the bow-string.

Drawing arm. The arm of the hand that draws the bow string.

Draw-weight. The strength of a bow when fully drawn measured in pounds at a specified draw length. Thus 50 lbs. at 28 inches.

Kenning. A conventional metaphoric name for an object. Such as Anglo Saxon *hildnaedre* 'battlesnake' for war-arrow.

Nocked. (Nocking) Fitting the arrow to the string in preparation for drawing and releasing.

Peck (marks). Dotted indentations made in a bow limb with the point of a chisel, forming various shapes.

Popinjay. A stylized representation of a parrot or a dove mounted on a pole as a target.

Riser. Correctly a wooden addition to the center of a bow for ease of grip. Also used to describe the increased depth of the central section.

Roving Marks. A number of man-made or natural features at which archers shot in sequence across open fields (roving).

Scarfing (in). Longitudinal joining of two pieces of wood—either as part of a bow, in manufacture, or as a replacement for damaged wood on a bow limb.

Self-yew. Said correctly of a bow made from a stave of only one type of wood. Now also taken to include two separate limbs of a single wood, spliced in the center.

Shaftment. That part of the arrow shaft on which the feathers are placed.

Side-nocked. A bow-string groove cut into the side of each horn bow tip, rather than around them.

Socketed. A type of arrow-head fixed by inserting the tapered cone of an arrow's end into its socket.

Stringing-horn. The correct name for the horn tip on a long bow's upper limb.

Tanged. A type of arrow-head fixed by insertion of a pointed tang into the end of an arrow shaft.

Tillering. A term applied to the careful checking of the bow limb curves using a 'tiller bar' on which the bow is held and bent.

Toxophilite. A lover of archery. Derived from Greek '*toxon*' bow, '*philus*' loving.

Trained Band. A local defense force of trained men. Militia.

Notes and References

CHAPTER ONE: STANCE AND POSTURE

1. The Luttrell Psalter was commissioned by Sir Geoffrey Luttrell, Lord of the Manor of Irnham, Lincolnshire, and it is believed was compiled between 1320, and 1340. Sir Geoffrey had it created to help with the provisions for his Will. It is embellished with many illustrations of middle English rural life, including archers at practice. This is of interest since it depicts shooting style, blunt arrowheads, and the shape of the contemporary butt. The arrowheads had small spikes to penetrate the Butt, but their blunt ends would have been ineffective against prey larger than birds or small mammals, thus safeguarding the King's deer.

2. Thorpe, *The Bayeux Tapestry and the Norman Invasion*. The Tapestry is thought by many to have been commissioned by Bishop Odo prior to 1077; it is housed in the Cathedral of Notre Dame, Bayeux.

3. Stein, *Archers d'Autrefois, Archers d'Aujourd'hui* for the account in medieval French. See also, *The Archer's Register*, 1902–3, 264–274, for an English version.

4. Henri de Ferrierre, *Livres du Roi Modus et de la Reine Ratio*, published in France between 1354 and 1376. *Modus* = mood and *Ratio* = reason. The work describes the hunting of various animals, distinguishing between those that are unpleasant (*Modus*), and those that are not (*Ratio*).

5. Gaston Phoebus, Comte du Fois. *Livre de Chasse*, published in France between 1387 and 1388. This work deals with the hunting of various animals while omitting the anthropomorphic distinctions made by de Ferrierre.

6. Ascham, *Toxophilius*.

7. Moseley, *An Essay on Archery*.

8. Raikes, *History of the Honourable Artillery Company*. There is some circumstantial evidence for an earlier origin of the Guild; the King's Roll of Payments contains certain entries between 1509 and 1515 of monies paid to the "Fraternity of Saint George's Guild."

9. Soar, "Prince Arthur's Knights," 31–39.

10. Neade, *The Double Armed Man by the New Invention*.

11. Markham, *The Art of Archery*.

12. Raikes, *History of the Honourable Artillery Company*, 153.

13. Heath, "The Antient Scorton Silver Arrow."

14. Soar, "Some Notes on the Regulations of Two Seventeenth Century Archery Societies," 8–12.

15. Paul, *History of the Royal Company of Archers.*
16. Moseley, *An Essay on Archery.*

Chapter Two: Lessons from Our Predecessors

1. Roberts, *The English Bowman.*
2. Niccols, *London Artillery.*
3. Raikes, *History of the Honourable Artillery Company,* Vol. 2, 104, et seq.
4. The Royal British Bowmen archery society was formed in 1787 and operated until 1794 when shooting ceased on the commencement of the Napoleonic campaign. Activity resumed briefly in the early 1800s but ceased shortly after. Full activity recommenced in 1818 and continued until 1880 when, in consideration of the premature death by drowning of the Patron's son, shooting ceased permanently.
5. A song composed by Mr Hayman at a Meeting of the Royal British Bowmen at Leeswood, July 23, 1819.

> In tracing the Society I find it first began
> Like Paradise of old with a woman and a man
> And contented they did go.
> This woman was a lady fair, and likewise wondrous civil,
> And to her came another man who prov'd a very devil,
> And a'walking they did go.
> He spoke to her of shafts and darts and wondrous stories told
> Of colors 'white', and 'black' & 'red' and then he talk'd of Gold.
> And a'tempting he did go.
> He swore if she'd adopt his plan, he'd much excel her name
> And what was more her own dear man sh'd not think her to blame

The Lady was Lady Cunliffe, wife of Sir Foster, the recorded Founder.
6. Woodmen Of Arden Records.
7. Waring, *A Treatise on Archery.*
8. Hargrove, *Anecdotes of Archery.* Fraternity of St George formed 1835. Rule XVII "That no person engaged in the trade of Bowyer or Fletcher, shall be admitted a member of this Society, or be allowed to shoot upon the Ground."
9. *The Archer's Register. A Year-Book of Facts*, published between 1864 and 1867, and again between 1876 and 1915. It drew together information from those archery clubs and Societies that chose to publish their competition results, and reflected views and material of interest to the archery fraternity of the United Kingdom and latterly of the United States of America. It closely followed information within *The Field* sporting newspaper with which it was closely associated.
10. The Leamington and Midland Counties Meeting was the first of the public meetings to be started after the Grand National. Three consecutive Grand Nationals had been held at York and it was determined that in addition to these, another annual event should be held, at Leamington. This was organized by N. Meridew, the secretary to the annual meeting, but supported enthusiastically by the Leamington bowyer Henry Bown. The first meeting

was held in 1854. Bown became secretary to the meeting in 1871 and continued in this position until 1884.

11. Aldred, *Young Archer's Assistant*. The "ardent admirer" was Francis Merewether who began his competitive archery career with the Herefordshire Bow Meeting in 1834, and with whom he shot intermittently until 1877. A summary of his activities within and outside archery can be found in Fox and Sinclair, *The Herefordshire Bowmeeting: A Social History*.

12. H. A. Ford, "The Theory and Practice of Archery," *Field*, October 6, 1855, subsequently expanded and published in 1856 as *Archery its Theory and Practice*. A recent discovery suggests that at least a part of chapter 5, "Of the Arrow," concerning the flight of the arrow when leaving the bow, was not written by Ford. In the *Field* sporting newspaper for August 3, 1861, the unknown contributor of an article "Theory of the Bow" identified only as "A. M." writes that: "My Theory of the Bow has nothing in common with the article in Mr. Ford's book which was written by two Cambridge men."

13. Ayres, *Handbook of Archery*.

14. H. D., *The Archers Guide*. Messrs Joseph, Myers & Co. were noted principally for their Educational Toys. The identity of "H. D." is unknown.

15. Walrond, *Archery for Beginners*.

16. *The United Bowmen of Philadelphia*. This was a limited edition of 200 copies. A copy was respectfully presented to Her Most Excellent Majesty Queen Elizabeth II who expressed her gratitude.

17. *Scribners Monthly Magazine*, Vol. XVI, May 1878, 8–9.

18. *The Archer's Register* 1879, 179. A summary of arrangements for the National contest. See also *The Archer's Register* 1880, 178–189 for a comprehensive list of competitors with scores and awards. Also details of the following Societies: Wabash Merry Bowmen; Oak Bow Club; Highland Park Archers; Desmoines Toxophilites; Buffalo Archery Society; Ohio State Tournament; and the Eastern Archery Association.

19. Expert, *The Archer's Complete Guide*. The expert is not identified.

20. Spencer, *The Spencer System of Shooting*.

CHAPTER THREE: HOLDING THE BOW, NOCKING, AND DRAWING

1. See Stein, *Archers d'Autrefois, Archers d'Aujourd'hui* for the account in medieval French. See also *The Archer's Register*, 1902–3, 264–274 for an English version.

2. Cadet, *Shooting Technique for Competition*.

3. Ritson, *Robin Hood, Poems, Songs and Ballads*.

> Robin Hode and the Potter (second fytte).
> Now schall I wet (know) an (if) thou be good.
> And polle (pull) het (it) op to thy ner(thine ear)
> So God me helpe, sayde the proude potter,
> This is but ryghyt weke ger (gear)

4. Soar, "Notes within *The English Bowman*," 64–75.

5. Ibid.

6. Dixon, *The Archer's Guide.*

7. Pownall, *Archery Records (Ford's scores excluded).* See page 4 for his explanation of the omission of scores made by H. A. Ford.

8. It is customary to speak of the commercially made steel bow as originating in Sweden in the 1930s. This improperly dismisses the "Badger" steel bow made and marketed briefly in the United States by one Mr. Badger in 1880.

CHAPTER FOUR: THE AIM, THE SIGHT, AND THE LOOSE

1. Herrigel, *Zen in the Art of Archery.* Speaking of the loose, the Zen Master reproves: "You feel it because you have not really let go of yourself. It is all so simple. You can learn from an ordinary bamboo leaf what ought to happen. It bends lower and lower under the weight of snow. Suddenly the snow slips to the ground, without the leaf knowing it. Stay like that at the point of highest tension until the snow falls from you. So, indeed it is: when the tension is fulfilled, the shot must fall. It must fall from the archer like snow from a bamboo leaf, before he even thinks of it."

2. City of London, Guildhall. "Be it remembered that this yere the fyrst day of the wrastlyng was chaunged into Games of Shotyng as here ys seen." There follows the arrangement for the days shooting. C.L.R.O. (City of London Record Office) Small MS. Box 1. No. 11.

3. Wood, *The Bowman's Glory, or Archery Revived.*

4. "R.S." [name unknown], *A Briefe Treatise.*

5. *Ayme for Finsburie Archers,* 1601.

6. Raikes, *History of the Honourable Artillery Company.* Vol. 2, 115 et seq.

7. *Archers of the City of London,* 1652. Manuscript booklet containing a list of Stewards of the Society of Finsbury Archers, and other varied information concerning the Society.

8. Ibid.

9. Soar, "The Catherine of Braganza Badge and other Society of Finsbury Archers Matters."

10. *The Ancient Honour of the Famous City of London Restored and Recovered by the Noble Sir John Robinson, Knight and Baronet, Lord Mayor for this year 1663.*

11. Soar, "Some Notes on the Regulations of Two Seventeenth Century Archery Societies," 8–11.

12. Hargrove, *Anecdotes of Archery,* 217–222.

13. Soar, "Notes within *The English Bowman*," 64–75.

14. Mason, *Pro Aris et Focis.*

15. Waring, *A Treatise on Archery. A recognition of the 'archer's paradox,'* 16.

16. *The Archer's Register,* 1898–99, "The Honest Archer," 275.

17. James Spedding (d. 1880) was an archer/coach born before his time. His problems and their prospective solutions were recognized not just by his contemporaries, but by those in other archery disciplines today. Among innovations which he created and explored were a built up handle made of gutta-percha, a malleable rubbery solution which hardened to give the desired shape. He was seemingly the only archer of any note who at that time used anything other than a point of aim.

18. Spencer, *The Spencer System of Shooting the Bow.* See chapter 23, "Aiming and Holding," and chapter 30, "Rigid Arrows," for brief commentary upon points of aim and "spine."

19. Lambert, *Modern Archery*, chapter 29, "Sighting Devices," chapter 30, "The Lambert Sight at Long Range," and chapter 27, "The Flight of the Arrow."

20. Ibid.

21. The Regulations for International Archery permitted, vide Article 27, "points of aim on the ground are allowed. Such 'points of aim' must not exceed a height of 6 inches. Other artificial aids to aiming are forbidden." This regulation was challenged in 1952 when an American motion, together with the president's proposal in favor of permitting pin-sights at world championship meetings, was rejected by six votes to five. However, in 1955, an article was added: "Simple bow-sights other than dioptric (lens) shall be allowed. Points of aim shall be allowed as now. Draw length indicators shall be allowed. An attachment to the string [a "kisser"] is also allowed."

CHAPTER FIVE: NECESSARY TACKLE

1. Hamer, *Anglo-Saxon Verse*, "The Battle of Maldon," line 110, *Bogan wearan bisige* (bows were busy); lines 265–273, in modern English, "The hostage started eagerly to help them. He was of bold Northumberland family. He never weakened in the battle-play, but sent forth arrows fast and continuously. Sometimes he struck a shield. Sometimes he pierced a man and constantly he gave some wound, as long as he survived to wield his weapon."

2. Hamer, *Anglo-Saxon Verse*, "Beowulf," lines 2435–2440, in modern English, "For the eldest unfittingly was the bed of death laid out by his kinsman's deed. Once from his horn-bow (hornbogan) Haethcyn killed him with an arrow, his noble loved one, he missed his mark and shot down his kinsman, his own brother with a bloody shaft."

3. *The Archer's Register,* 1912, "The Bows and Arrows of the Ancient Saxons," 241–246.

4. J. Bradbury, "The Battle of the Standard (Northallerton, Northumberland) 1138," in *The Medieval Archer*, 51–52, London, 1985. See also, *Henry of Huntingdon*, 262–270, facsimile, Llanerch Press, 1991.

5. "Turquoy bows of Stele;" if these bows were truly of steel, then the term turquy, turkie, turquoy, etc., may have a defined purpose in the context of hunting, a colloquial generic term for a particular weapon, as distinguished from a war bow. Equally it may have been an accepted colloquial term used before the now universal "long bow."

6. Gendall, "The Arundel Archive of Arrows and Arrow Heads." See also Hugh D. H. Soar, *Straight and True: A Select History of the Arrow*, 82–84.

7. "Weapons of Warre," Parts 1 and 2, *Archaeology of the* Mary Rose, Vol. 3, Chapter 8.

8. Wadge, *Arrowstorm*. Part 2. "The supply and manufacture of bows and arrows;" see especially appendix 3, "Bows and arrows received at the Tower of London, January 1355–February 1360."

9. In March 1371, representatives of both the Bowyers and the Fletchers of the city of London presented a petition to the Mayor and Aldermen asking that the two trades should be kept separate. This was granted and thus the two worshipful companies came into existence. Subsequently, in 1987, a craft guild of traditional bowyers and fletchers was formed modeled on the lines of the ancient companies, and although these companies are no longer associated with their ancient crafts, a close link has developed between each and the new craft guild.

10. Jessop, "A New Artefact Typology for the study of Medieval Arrowheads." Unlike the London Museum catalogue which uses actual artifacts, in the new typology arrowheads with similar traits have been amalgamated and are divided into four generic forms. These are further subdivided into four broad groups: target, multi-purpose, military, and hunting.

11. See Note 7. "Weapons of Warre." Part 2. Hugh D. H. Soar, "Bracers."

12. Leach, "The Renishaw Bow known as Robin Hood's Bow," 11–18.

13. *The Ancient Vellum Book of the Honourable Artillery Company.* Entry for Thomas Rodes, September 15, 1680.

14. Paul, *History of the Royal Company of Archers.* Appendix, 371, Athole, December 1, 1778.

15. Ibid. Appendix, 369. Simon Fraser. Writer to the signet. August 11, 1770. Hugh Fraser of Lovett, Appendix, 366.

16. Ibid., 126. "After his being made Praeses, Dr Spens does not seem to have attended any Meetings of the Company: but in 1810 he gave a bow to be shot for, and in that year he was entertained at dinner on the sixtieth anniversary of his admission as a member."

17. Soar, "John Spreat, a Bath Bowyer of the 1820s." Contains a select biography.

18. "Archery," *Badminton Library*, London, 1884.

19. P. Muir Letter to the Editor. *Field*, December 24, 1864, concerning the newly patented Alexandra Arrow. Extract: "This is no invention and therefore can have no patent rights. I made and experimented with such more than thirty years ago. I have no remembrance in what these experiments resulted, but believe they must have been unsatisfactory, inasmuch as the screw was not adopted. . . . I would conclude by remarking that had Dr Croft [patentee] known something more of an arrow, its use and history, he might have saved himself the expense of a Patent." See also, Soar, *Straight and True*.

20. M. Thompson, "Merry Days with Bow and Quiver," *Scribners Monthly*, Vol. XVI, No. 1 (May 1878). Extracts: (p. 5) "Of course after a little practice we will easily find the target's Gold, with the light, beautiful arrows of Mr. Highfield" (p. 14); "I am speaking of those beautiful and valuable things made by Mr. Highfield." M. Thompson, *Witchery of Archery*, 1879 edition, 238: "I have found the yellow coloured lemonwood bows of Highfeld's much the best to stand all kinds of usage, but the snakewood, yew, lancewood and the backed bows are the springier and quicker."

21. M. Thompson, "Horsman's Catalog," May 1879. "I can recommend your bows as more durable and better finished than English bows of the same material."

Chapter Six: Of Targets and Scoring

1. Dobson and Taylor, *Rymes of Robyn Hood*. "A geste of Robin Hod—seventh fitte," verses 395–410.
2. J. Ritson, *Robin Hood, Poems, Songs and Ballads*. "Robin Hood and Queen Catherine," verses 235–243.
3. See Note 1. "Robin Hood and the Monk," verses 10–15.
4. *Ayme for Finsburie Archers*, 1601.
5. Partridge, *Ayme for Finsburie Archers*, London, 1628.
6. Shotterel and Durfey, *The Bowman's Excellence: a Poem*. Appendix, "Orders and observations touching the Noble Exercise of Shooting the Longbow to be observed by those which practise the noble art."
7. Roberts, *The English Bowman*, chapter 10, "Roving," 230–235.
8. *Records of the Woodmen of Arden 1785–1985*, Appendix 2.
9. *Rules of the British Longbow Society*.
10. Scot, *Discoverie of Witchcraft*, 52.
11. *The Royal Toxophilite Society*.
12. Waring, *Treatise of Archery*, 37–42.
13. De Bertier, *Cordier et Guglielmini*, "Le Tir a l' Arc."
14. Hargrove, *Anecdotes of Archery*, 160–166.
15. Ibid., 72–77.
16. *The Archer's Register*, 1885–86. "Song of the arrow boy," anon., 63. See also, *The Archer's Register*, 1884–85, "The Archery Judge."

Chapter Seven: A Matter of Style

1. *Book of Reckonings and other Memoranda 1500-1612*. Extracts from the "Muster Book of Shere," 1583, 20. "Archers selected 10. Archers of the best sort 2. Archers of the second sort 5." Although the billmen in the same muster were named, the archers were not.
2. Hansard, *The Book of Archery*, 56–57. Hansard quotes a poem by Carrell in which an archer called Black Will boasts of killing Lord Lisle. Another account by Leland in his "itinerary" (reprinted in 1769 from the original MS in the Bodleian), however, states that the assassin's name was James Hyatte.
3. The Sixth Sermon preached before King Edward, April 12, 1549: "In my time my poor father was as diligent to teach me to shoot, as to learn me any other thing; and so I think other men did their children. He taught me how to draw, how to lay my body in my bow, and not to draw with strength of arms, as other nations do, but with strength of the body: I had my bows bought me, according to my age and strength; as I increased in them, so my bows were made bigger and bigger, for men shall never shoot well, except they be brought up in it: it is a goodly art, a wholesome kind of exercise, and much commended in physic."
4. Ascham, *Toxophilus*, 194.

5. Ibid., 194-195.

6. Waring, *A Treatise on Archery*, 14.

7. "Archery," *Badminton Library*, 385.

8. Ford, *Archery, Its Theory and Practice*.

9. Ibid., 80.

10. See note 3 above.

11. Ritson, *Robin Hood. Poems, Songs and Ballads*, 90.

12. Herrigel, *Zen in the Art of Archery*, 45.

13. Hansard, *The Book of Archery*, 55. Hansard commenting in a footnote on an archer guard, half of whom were left-handed, in order to protect their sultan from both sides says, "A bowman left handed is undoubtedly the most ungainly of monsters, to whom the recommendation of even so grave an authority as Plato fails to reconcile us. The Greek philosopher considered that children should be taught to use both hands with equal dexterity . . . for among the Scythians, he says, men draw the bow equally with both hands. I repeat however, that it has a very contemptible appearance and is unpardonable because any one may cure himself of the bad habit in a week."

14. Thompson, *The Witchery of Archery*, 264. Thompson indicates that the rules of the Derby & Reddlestone (sic) archers which he lists on page 261, had been "in substance" adopted by the Wabash Merry Bowmen. It is not clear which club the rules on the following pages belong to as they bear little relationship to each other; and in particular one which states, "that no archer shall be allowed on the grounds if he is known to shoot left handed," does not appear at all in the Derby rules shown. It can only be assumed that pages 262, 263, and 264—including the left-handed rule—apply to the Wabash Merry Bowmen.

Bibliography

Aldred, Thomas. *The Young Archer's Assistant. Being an Introduction into the art of shooting with the bow by a practical and ardent admirer of that Noble Pastime.* London: privately published, 1854.

The Ancient Honour of the Famous City of London Restored and Recovered by the Noble Sir John Robinson, Knight and Baronet, Lord Mayor for this year 1663. An account of Archery, Wrestling and Sword and Dagger play. London: City of London Record Office, Guildhall.

The Ancient Vellum Book of the Honourable Artillery Company, being the roll of Members from 1611 to 1682. Facsimile. London: G. Raikes, 1890.

Archers of the City of London. London: Privately published, 1652.

The Archer's Complete Guide, or Instruction for the use of the Long Bow. New York: Peck and Snyder, 1878.

The Archer's Complete Manual, or the art of shooting with the long-bow as practised by the United Bowmen of Philadelphia. Philadelphia: Privately published, 1830.

The Archer's Register. A Year-Book of Facts. London, 1864–1867; 1876–1915.

Ascham, Roger. *Toxophilus. The Schole or Positions of Shootynge.* 1544. Reprint. Wakefield, England: S.R. Publishers, in collaboration with the Society of Archer Antiquaries and the Grand National Archery Society.

Ayme for Finsburie Archers, or an Alphabetical Table of the names of everie Mark within the same fielde, with their true distances both by the Map and dimensuration by the line. London, 1601. Reprint, STC 1 Reel 2000. Ann Arbor, MI: University Micro Films.

Ayres, Frederick Henry. *A Handbook of Archery. Containing all information essentially required for the attainment of practical excellence in the ancient and noble science of shooting with the English Long Bow.* London: Privately published, 1898.

Book of Reckonings and other Memoranda 1500–1612. Shere: Church of St James.

Bradbury, Jim. *The Medieval Archer.* Stroud, UK: Sutton, 1985.

Cadet, J. *Shooting Technique for Competition. Rational Methods for Synchronised Automated Action.* Montreuil, France: Privately published, 1987. Translated from the French *Technique de Tir de Competition.*

Chesney, H. H. McC. *Archery, an Illustrated Treatise on Archery.* Minneapolis, MN, 1896.

De Bertier, *Cordier, et Guglielmini. Le Tir a l'Arc.* Paris, 1900.

Dixon, Hezekiah. *The Archer's Guide with Full Instruction for the use of the Long Bow. Illustrated with Plates shewing the positions in which the bow should be held.* London, 1853. Reprint. Machynlleth, Wales: Dyfi Valley Bookshop, 2003.

Dobson, R. B. and J. Taylor. *Rymes of Robin Hood.* London, 1976.

Elmer, Robert Potter. *The United Bowmen of Philadelphia.* Privately published: Philadelphia, U.S.A.

Ferrierre, Henri de. *Livres du Roi Modus et de Reine Ratio.* English translation Gunnar Tilander, Paris, 1932.

Ford, Horace Alfred. *Archery, its Theory and Practice.* London: Buchanan, 1856.

Fox, R. W. and J. Sinclair. *The Herefordshire Bowmeeting: A Social History.* Privately published, 2000.

Gendall, J. "The Arundel Archive of Arrows and Arrow Heads." *Journal of the Society of Archer Antiquaries,* Vol. 44 (2001) and Vol. 48 (2005).

Hamer, Richard. *Anglo-Saxon Verse.* London: Faber and Faber, 1970.

Hansard, George Agar. *The Book of Archery.* London: Longman & Co., 1841.

Hargrove, Alfred Edward. *Anecdotes of Archery from the earliest age to the year 1791 by the late E. Hargrove reviewed to include every Society of Archers.* York: Privately published, 1845.

H. D. *The Archers Guide, or Instructions for the use of the Long Bow.* London: A. N. Myers & Co, 1855.

Heath, E. G. "The Antient Scorton Silver Arrow." *Society of Archer Antiquaries.* London: privately published, 1972.

Henry of Huntingdon. Reprint. Llanerch Press, 1991.

Herrigel, Eugen. *Zen in the Art of Archery.* London: Routledge Kegan Paul, 1953.

Hildred, Alexzandra, ed. Weapons of Warre. "The Armaments of the Mary Rose." *The Archaeology of the* Mary Rose, Vol. 3. Portsmouth: Mary Rose Trust, 2011.

Hird, Ben. *The Antient Scorton Silver Arrow. Journal of the Society of Archer Antiquaries.* London: privately published, 1972.

Jessop, O. "A New Artefact Typology for the Study of Medieval Arrowheads." *Medieval Archaeology,* Vol XL, 1996.

Lambert, A. J., Jr. *Modern Archery.* New York: Barnes and Company, 1932.

Leach, M. "The Renishaw Bow known as Robin Hood's Bow." *Journal of the Society of Archer Antiquaries*, Vol. 54, 2011.

Longman C. J. and H. Walrond. "Archery." *The Badminton Library.* London, 1894.

Markham, Gervase. *The Art of Archery.* London, 1864. Reprint.

Mason, Oswald J. *Pro Aris et Focis. Considerations of the reasons that exist for Reviving the use of the Long Bow with the Pike.* London, 1798. Reprint. London: Tabard Press, 1970.

Mitchell, T. S. *Archery.* Spalding's Athletic Library. Vol 4. No. 40. American Sports Publishing Co, 1895.

Moseley, Walter Michael Mitchell. *An Essay on Archery describing the Practice of that Art in all Ages and Nations.* Worcester: T. & T. Holl, 1792.

Myers, A. M. *The Archers Guide.* London: Privately published, 1855.

Neade, William. *The Double Armed Man, by the New Invention.* London, 1625. Reprint. York, PA: George Shumway, 1971.

Niccols, Richard. *London Artillery, briefly continuing the noble practice of that worldly Societie, with the modern and ancient martiall exercise, natures of armes, vertues of magistrates, glorie and chronography of his honourable cittie.* London: Privately published, 1616.

Partridge, J. *Ayme for Finsburie Archers.* London, 1628. Reprint. Royal Leamington Spa: W. C. Books, 1998.

Paul, James Balfour. *History of the Royal Company of Archers.* Edinburgh: William Blackwood, 1875.

Poebus, Gaston. *Livre de Chasse.* English translation Gunnar Tilander, Paris, 1932.

Pownall, Charles. *Archery Records (Ford's scores excluded). Made in the single York, National, Hereford and other Special Rounds at the Public and Club Meetings, including the various Distance Records both in Scores and Hits, together with an introductory Chapter and Notes and Reminiscences.* Woking: Privately printed, 1929.

Pratt, C. E., Ed. *Bicycling World and Archery Field.* Philadelphia, 1880.

Raikes, G. A. *The Ancient Vellum Book of the Honourable Artillery Company.* London, 1890.

Raikes, G. A. *History of the Honourable Artillery Company.* 2 volumes. London: R. Bentley and Son, 1878.

Records of the Woodmen of Arden 1785–1985. Banbury: Privately printed, 1986.

Ritson, Joseph. *Robin Hood's Poems, Songs and Ballads: A Collection of All the Ancient Poems, Songs and Ballads Now Extant, relative to That Celebrated English Outlaw to which are prefixed Historical Anecdotes of His Life.* London: John C. Nimmo, 1885.

Roberts, Thomas. *The English Bowman.* London, 1802. Reprint. Wakefield: EP Publishing, 1973.

The Royal Toxophilite Society. Edited by "A Toxophilite." London: Privately printed, 1867.

Rules of the British Longbow Society. Privately printed.

S. R. [Author unknown.] *A Briefe Treatise. To prove the necessitie and excellence of the use of Archerie, abstracted out of Ancient and Moderne Writers.* London, 1596.

Scot, Reginald. *Discoverie of Witchcraft, proving the common opinions of witches contracting with devils, spirits, or familiars.* London, 1651.

Shotterel, Robert and Thomas Durfey. *The Bowman's Excellence.* London, 1676.

Soar, Hugh D. H. "The Catherine of Braganza Badge and Other Society of Finsbury Archers Matters." *Journal of the Society of Finsbury Archers,* Vol. 56. Privately published, 2013.

_____. *The Crooked Stick: A History of the Longbow.* Yardley, PA: Westholme Publishing, 2005.

_____. "John Spreat, a Bath Bowyer of the 1820s." *Journal of the Society of Archer Antiquaries,* No. 34, 1993.

_____. "Notes within *The English Bowman.*" *Journal of the Society of Archer Antiquaries.* London: Privately published, 2002.

_____. "Prince Arthur's Knights: Some Notes on a Sixteenth Century Society of Archers." *Journal of the Society of Archer Antiquaries.* London: Privately published, 1983.

_____. *The Romance of Archery: A Social History of the Longbow.* Yardley, PA: Westholme Publishing, 2008.

_____. "Some Notes on the Regulations of Two Seventeenth Century Archery Societies." *Journal of the Society of Archer Antiquaries.* London: Privately published, 1992.

_____. *Straight and True: A Select History of the Arrow.* Yardley, PA: Westholme Publishing, 2010.

Soar, Hugh D. H., with Joseph Gibbs, Christopher Jury, and Mark Stretton. *Secrets of the English War Bow.* Yardley, PA: Westholme Publishing, 2006.

Spencer, Stanley. *The Spencer System of Shooting.* Albany, OR: Privately published, 1933.

Stein, Henri. *Archers de'Autrefois et du Aujourd'hui.* Paris, 1925.

Thompson, Maurice. *The Witchery of Archery.* 1879. Reprint.

Thompson, Maurice and Will Thompson. *How to Train in Archery.* New York: E. I. Horsman, 1879. Reprint.

Thorpe, L. *The Bayeux Tapestry and the Norman Invasion.* London: Folio Society, 1973.

The United Bowmen of Philadelphia 1828–1953. A 125th anniversary commemoration. Philadelphia: Privately published, 1953.

Wadge, Richard. *Arrowstorm: The World of the Archer in the Hundred Years War.* London: Stroud, 2007.

Walker, G. Gould. *History of the Honourable Artillery Company.* Aldershot: Dale and Polden, 1954.

Walrond, H. *Archery for Beginners.* London, 1904. Reprint, London: Phillips Hereford, 1935.

Waring. Thomas (the Younger). *A Treatise on Archery, or the Art of Shooting with the Long Bow, containing every requisite information to obtain a complete knowledge of the Noble Weapon, considered an Instrument of Amusement. Likewise a Dissertation on the steel crossbow, with directions for using it. To which is added a Summary Sketch of laws for Archers with many other Observations and Instructions.* London: privately published, 1814.

Waring. Thomas (the Younger). *A Treatise on Archery. A recognition of the archer's 'paradox', with an attempted geometric explanation, omitting reference to the effect of 'spine' or stiffness of the arrow.* London: privately published, 1814.

Wood, William. *The Bowman's Glory, or Archery Revived, giving an Account of the many signal Favours vouchsafed to Archers and Archery by those renowned monarchs, King Henry VIII, James I, Charles I. Includes the Patent of Henry VIII concerning archery (Fraternity of St George), and A Remembrance of the worthy Show and Shooting by the Duke of Shoreditch and his Associates, the Worshipful Citizens of London.* London, 1682. Reprint. Wakefield: S.R. Publishers in collaboration with the Society of Archer Antiquaries and the Grand National Archery Society, 1969.

"Woodmen Of Arden Records." London: Privately published, 1885, 1935, 1985, and 2010.

Acknowledgments

I acknowledge with grateful thanks the advice and help given me by my publisher, Bruce H. Franklin, whose idea for this book it was. I thank my wife and partner Veronica-Mae for patiently adjusting my wayward syntax, and in particular for her masterly contribution of chapter seven ably aided by friend and fine photographer Elisabeth Allen.

I must also acknowledge with gratitude the numerous experts whose trenchant advice across the centuries will have helped some and bewildered others. I single out for especial mention, philosopher and toxophilite Roger Ascham, analytical theorist Horace Ford, and the unequivocal Stanley Spencer. There have been many others.